EMBLEMS OF MORTALITY

Iconographic Experiments in Shakespeare's Theatre

Clayton G. MacKenzie

University Press of America, Inc.
Lanham • New York • Oxford

Copyright © 2000 by
University Press of America,® Inc.
4720 Boston Way
Lanham, Maryland 20706

12 Hid's Copse Rd.
Cumnor Hill, Oxford OX2 9JJ

Library of Congress Cataloging-in-Publication Data

MacKenzie, Clayton G.
Emblems of mortality : iconographic experiments in Shakespeare's theatre /
Clayton G. MacKenzie
p. cm.
Includes bibliographical references and index.
1. Shakespeare, William, 1564-1616—Criticism and interpretation.
2. Death in literature. 3. Art and literature—England—History—
16th century. 4. Art and literature—England—History—17th century. 5.
Shakespeare, William, 1564-1616—Knowledge—Art. 6. Death in art.
I. Title
PR3069.D42 M33   2000   822.3'3—dc21   00-023148 CIP

)-7618-1660-7 (cloth: alk. ppr.)

⊖™ The paper used in this publication meets the minimum
requirements of American National Standard for Information
Sciences—Permanence of Paper for Printed Library Materials,
ANSI Z39.48—1984

In memory of my mother

Wendy Joy MacKenzie

1929-1999

Contents

List of Plates

Acknowledgments

All research is to a greater or lesser extent collaborative, and it is certainly a pleasure to begin by acknowledging the great debt I owe to students and colleagues whose questions and insights illuminated my thinking in the years before and after I began writing this book. Eleanor Porter looked at an early draft of the manuscript and, in her unassuming and tactful way, turned me in some of the directions I needed to go. Peter Stambler read a later version and brought to it his immense intellect, as well as a poetic intuition for balance and meaning. Aside from her professional excellence, my research assistant, Annie Cheng, was also an invaluable source of enthusiasm and good humor. Stuart Christie fine-tuned some of my thinking in the last stages of preparation, and I benefited from both his wisdom and his wit.

My work took me to churches, cathedrals, palaces, stately homes, archives, and libraries in many parts of England and, on a couple of occasions, in continental Europe and the United States. To the dozens of people who helped me, many of them anonymously, I offer my gratitude. I am particularly indebted to Julie Coleman in the Department of Special Collections at Glasgow University Library, to Lori Johnson at the Folger Shakespeare Library, and to the staff at the British Library. The inter-library loan personnel at Hong Kong Baptist University Library were superb in their efficiency and professionalism—unfailingly courteous and forever determined to help. At the publication stage of the book, the staff at the University Press of America labored tirelessly on my behalf, answering my many questions, suggesting modifications, and generally being the kind of friends that every writer needs. I am especially obliged to Helen Hudson, the production editor, and to Peter Cooper, the managing editor.

Hong Kong Baptist University funded research trips to Europe in 1996, 1998, and 1999, and gave me every support, material and moral, in my efforts to complete this book. My special thanks go to Jane Lai, Terry Yip, Frank Fu and Björn Jernudd whose unrelenting endeavors on my behalf afforded me both the time and the resources to bring this project to fruition. I gained enormously from my links with the drama department at Sha Tin College, learning much from the wonderful tradition of Renaissance theatre that Flikki Lapish and her colleagues have developed there over the last decade. Nicole Ho, Carina Lok, Dorothy Albritton, Rebecca and Simon Brown, and Pilar Wyman gave generously of their time during the preparation of the final manuscript. Finally, I owe a great debt to my wife, Moira, for her unstinting support and advice; and to our four children (Odette, aged 4; Alistair and Conor, aged 2; and Piers, aged 1), who did all in their power to stop me writing this book and, in the process, helped me to keep in perspective the really important bits of life.

A few of the chapters have been developed out of previous journal publications. Chapter 2 is partly derived from my 1986 article in *Shakespeare Quarterly*. Chapter 3 is loosely based on articles that appeared in *Neohelicon* and in *AUMLA*, both published in 1995.

Clayton G. MacKenzie
Kowloon Tong
Christmas 1999

Chapter 1

℘ℛ

Introduction

The word "mortality" derives from the Latin *mortalis*, meaning death. When Adam and Eve, in the Biblical garden, somehow conspired to eat the forbidden fruit, they threw away eternity. Until then, there was to be no death. In a state of unequivocal bliss, the pair would live for ever, the immortal inhabitants of Eden. But they transgressed, and their punishment was not only expulsion from paradise but the loss of immortality. Henceforth, they and their descendants would grow old and physically expire. They would become subject to the trials and temptations of transient life: sinning, atoning, fearing, celebrating, hating, loving, mourning, dying. The full compendium of human potential and ignominy, triumph and mundanity and despair, would be theirs. To us, of their trace, such punishment for first offenders may seem harsh but God had his reasons. This was no ordinary crime. It was the first crime, the father of all crimes; every crime that followed in every age that followed emanated from it. The human condition, perhaps more varied than it would have been without transgression, was also infinitely more terrifying. The cruel cycle of birth, flowering, withering and death reiterated itself relentlessly and without exception, the transient pleasures of bliss forever blighted by the certitude of the grave.

Mortality means death; but it also means a quality of life. It stands
for the full gamut of human experience, those achievements and failings
that distinguish every age of human endeavor in a postlapsarian world.
Shakespeare understood and used both meanings but, if usage is an arbiter
of intent, his text shows a preference for the idea of mortality as the
condition of life in a world where all living things will die. Such is the
king's meaning in *Henry V* when he scorns war as a "waste in brief
mortality" (I.i.28).[1] And such is Pericles' sense when, realizing his
daughter is alive and well, he cries out

> Give me a gash, put me to present pain,
> Lest this great sea of joys rushing upon me
> O'erbear the shores of my mortality,
> And drown me with their sweetness.
> *(Pericles* V.i.191-4)

Fifteenth and sixteenth century Europe regarded its own mortality
with a curious mix of regret and pride. Regret, of course, because the
mortal state was so self-evidently prone to corruption and decline; but
pride, too, because out of this miasma of transgressive error, humanity
had yet been able to manipulate its world and to create from it that which
was both admirable and enduring. Possibly for this reason, the temptation
of Adam and Eve is often presented ambivalently. True, there is a
devious serpent about the place. But there is often, also, a handsome
couple, perhaps too attractively fleshed, and a tree replete with overly-
succulent fruits. I cannot recall a portraiture that opted for sagging
buttocks and maggot-ridden apples. It is an ambivalence that did not
escape the attention of Oliver Cromwell, whose parliament met for a
time in the circular Chapter House at Salisbury Cathedral. In a wonderful
Medieval frieze that encircles the room, the books of the Old Testament
are summarized in Purbeck marble. The section pertaining to Adam and
Eve's temptation in Genesis is a modern replica since the original was
held to be just a little too delicious for God-fearing men, and fell to the
chisels of the Lord Protector's artisans. Nonetheless, this most popular
of Biblical emblems survived in many other locations and genres, as, for
example, in an alluringly vivid nave boss high in the roof of Norwich
Cathedral, recently brought to wider public attention through the
photographs of Julia Hedgecoe, and in the smooth seductiveness of a
carved arm chair in the White Bear Inn which housed the workmen who

constructed and repaired Salisbury Cathedral (*plate 1*). The world, fallen perhaps, still offered an enchanting landscape.

Humankind, in its postlapsarian state, had much to lament; but long before Shakespeare came to write, it also felt it had much to celebrate. From the European Middle Ages many great systems for ordering the affairs of human beings had emerged or consolidated themselves: constitutional monarchy; parliaments; the seats of learning at Bologna, Paris, Oxford, and Cambridge; trial by jury; the Roman Catholic Church. To these, the early and middle Renaissance had added astonishing advances in sciences and arts, and had thrown up individuals of extraordinary daring and vitality. Protestantism came; feudalism mostly went; the "known" world quadrupled in size. Few ages have experienced such dramatic alterations in the circumstances of human life and in the possibilities it offered. But though the world was changing, and many supposed that change was for the better, the familiar failings of human nature, the behest of that early transgression, continued to manifest themselves.

* * * * *

The Elizabethans were sharply aware of the shortcomings and celebrations of the world they inhabited, and much of what they wrote or sculpted or painted engaged these very issues. In the early sixteenth century an elaborate ritualization of the journey from birth to death began to evolve, endorsed by a rich culture of visual art and artifacts. Whereas in our own age the engagement with death has been discretely narrowed into a brief process of formal commemoration and burial, by Shakespeare's time it was ritualized into the very fabric of everyday life. The reminders of death, the journey to the grave, the moment of expiry — these were all very central to the cultural engagement with mortality in post-Reformation England, and not at all marginalized as they often are today. Inevitably, this way of seeing the world influenced the writings of Shakespeare and his contemporaries, not only in relation to the intellectual content of the drama but with regard to its visual impressions as well. Death came to be regarded not simply as the moment when physical life expires but as an elaborate social ceremonial in which the individual was invited both to imagine and contemplate death from the earliest years of his or her sentient life. The purposes of this ritualization were not always clear and often bizarre, but its existence impacted powerfully on Shakespeare's age. Its effects were not only reflected in the tensions and interplays of the text itself, but were often expressed visually through theatrical emblematizations.

There is now a fairly extensive literature dealing with early modern representations of death, with several important publications in the last few years (for example: Michael Neill's *Issues of Death: Mortality and Identity in English Renaissance Tragedy* (1997)), building on the seminal writings of Philippe Ariès, Theodore Spencer, Harry Morris, R. M. Frye, James Calderwood, Phoebe Spinrad, Kirby Farrell, Michael Cameron Andrews, Julian Litten, and Arnold Stein. A number of works have been especially relevant to the present study. Roland Mushat Frye's *The Renaissance Hamlet: Issues and Responses in 1600* (1984) has offered detailed commentary on Elizabethan attitudes towards death, and explored funerary practices and *memento mori* conventions. Its influence on the present study has extended beyond the discussion of *Hamlet*. Harry Morris' *Last Things in Shakespeare* (1985) maps Shakespeare's eschatology — an eschatology inherited, as Morris demonstrates, from sources as diverse as Prudentius' *Psychomachia* and the *Queen Elizabeth Prayer Book* — through both tragedy and comedy. Kirby Farrell's essay on *Romeo and Juliet* in *Play, Death, and Heroism in Shakespeare* (1987) provides a stimulating and challenging psychoanalytical reading of Shakespeare's theatre and has been particularly helpful in its engagement of issues pertaining to love and death. Patricia L. Carlin in *Shakespeare's Mortal Men: Overcoming Death in History, Comedy and Tragedy* (1993) has considered the confrontation between life and death in a number of Shakespearean texts, tracing the conflict to Medieval theatre and, like Farrell, focusing most usefully on matters of love and death. In another intriguing psychological study, *The Rest is Silence: Death as Annihilation in the English Renaissance* (1994), Robert Watson has suggested that the suspicion that death meant annihilation drove Renaissance culture into crisis, a state recognizable, he demonstrates, in Elizabethan theatre. William E. Engel in *Mapping Mortality: The Persistence of Memory and Melancholy in Early Modern England* (1995) argues for a connection between mnemonics and death (and Death, the allegorical figure), showing how everyday metaphoric structures in the Renaissance could often be construed as fleeting revelations of death (and of allegorical Death). Michael Neill's *Issues of Death: Mortality and Identity in English Renaissance Tragedy* (1997) affords the reader a rich repository of information on and analysis of early modern attitudes towards death and burial, relating these cogently to the theatre. Two works not specifically located in the literary domain have been notably helpful: Nigel Llewellyn's monograph *The Art of Death: Visual Culture in the English Death Ritual 1500-1800* (1991) is an invaluable guide to attitudes and practices in relation to death in the Renaissance; and Alastair Fowler's *Time's Purpled Masquers: Stars and the Afterlife in Renaissance English Literature* (1996) presents a concise overview of eschatological significances in the sixteenth century.

In *Emblems of Death*, three distinct *topoi* of mortality are considered in relation to Shakespeare's drama: life-in-death; *memento mori*; and *de morte et amore*. The first of these *topoi*, "life-in-death," is explored in Chapters 2 and 3. The idea of life-in-death was variously represented as a plant growing out of a skull or plants seeding bones or infants leaning nonchalantly on death's heads (see *plate 2*). The original meaning was clearly religious (spiritual life through physical death) but the humanizing inclinations of the sixteenth century emblematists, and the Elizabethan theatre, gradually renovated and secularized the familiar icons — ultimately proposing the defeat of death through the physical and spiritual regeneration of splendid mortality. In Shakespeare's History plays "rebirth" thus comes to mean physical procreation; and "spirituality" signifies a quality of heroic military conduct. Death, the physical moment, is inescapable; and its circumvention is perceived not in terms of a religious afterlife but with regard to a process of recurring familial greatness, achieved through successful militaristic forays abroad and the preservation of peace at home. The inevitability of natural death is thus moderated by the potential of youth, and the path to immortality is mapped through the regeneration of English chivalric excellence in foreign climes. It is argued that this attempt to subvert the dominion of death fails for two reasons: firstly, because historically the regeneration of evils in this period of English history, as recorded in Shakespeare's sources, was even more virulent than the regeneration of magnificences; and, secondly, because the very substance of regeneration (the conquest and killing of foreigners) gradually fell into disrepute as Shakespeare unfolded the English encomium.

The second species of emblem, the *mors/amor* conjunction, draws on the ancient relationship between love and death, and is examined in Chapter 4. Icons of skeletal Death are presented in relation to marital or romantic situations, and emblems of love (such as Cupid) have appended to them an unnerving capacity for death (see *plate 3*). In fusing the tenderness of love with the carnality of Death, these images sought to present love and death as part of a single cultural process — an idea dating back to antiquity but harnessed by Medieval eschatology into a divine scheme of judgment and punishment. And so in *Romeo and Juliet* where the forces of authority, who come to symbolize the judgement of death, attempt to stifle romantic love through the threat of death (as if somehow one is punishment for the other), it is left for the lovers themselves to reaffirm the symbiotic relation between the two. This they do through the mimicking of death, an extraordinary process culminating with Juliet seemingly dead in the Capulet tomb and Romeo approaching her corpse like a *danse macabre* figure threatening to kill everything in his path. At the play's end, the customary separation associated with the idea of physical death (the separation of lovers; the disjunction between life and the tomb) is disavowed, and death is reinstated as a social reality — a force neither to be embraced nor repelled, merely accepted as an imponderable factor of everyday mortality.

The third of the *topoi*, centering on the *memento mori* tradition and the focus of Chapters 5 and 6, considers intellectual engagement with death as a means of circumventing its physical terrors. In order to remember death, and to commemorate the lives of those who had already died, the sixteenth century developed a startling culture of deathly artifact (see *plate 4*). Tomb pendants with skeletonized interiors, marble skulls on funerary monuments, death's head ale mugs — everyday life was permeated with such objects, each attesting to the open socialization of death in Shakespeare's age. This forthrightness is evident in the theatre, and particularly in *Hamlet* where the young hero's intellectual duels with death — be it death the ghost, or death the skull, or death the young Laertes, or death the "fell sergeant" — articulate an elaborate and ritualized journey to the grave in which intellectual understanding stands as a kind of academicized riposte to the physical horrors of rotting mortality. Can death's sting be expurgated by contemplation? Perhaps yes, for while young Hamlet may balk at the putrefying reality of Yorick's skull, by the end of the play he has come sufficiently to terms with the idea of mortality to look upon the face of death with a certain equanimity, neither dissolving into the convulsive horror of emblem book victims nor disintegrating into the tardy piety of the supplicants on so many funereal monuments. The *danse macabre*, perhaps the most dramatic form of *memento mori*, was well known to Shakespeare and is referred to frequently in his work. In three plays — *Richard II*, *King John*, and *Coriolanus* — Shakespeare experiments with the dance of death as a theatrical device, articulating and flexing its potential as an emblematic counterpoint to the meaning of his plays. The encounter with the dance of death in these works reveals Death in various guises, and the significances attending each are not necessarily uniform. Skeletal death can be grim and terrifying, but also occasionally admirable, and even, at times, desirable.

All of the iconographic illustrations used in this book are selected from a Medieval or sixteenth century English context or from continental traditions known to have been popular in Renaissance England. I have drawn widely, but by no means exclusively, on a populist genre called the emblem book which emerged in the early part of the sixteenth century and sought to remind an age increasingly confident in its own worth and achievement that certain values and tenets remained pivotal to the progress of civilization. Typically, but not exclusively, a tripartite mix of picture, moral epigram and motto, these works acquired an astonishing popularity across Europe from the 1530s onwards, appearing in a dozen different languages and elevating to celebrity status some of the authors and engravers who created them. Other visual sources to which I have turned include illuminated manuscripts, funereal iconographies, and church and cathedral art. In considering Shakespeare's text, I wanted to work with the kinds of artistic impressions that, in all likelihood, would have formed part of the *direct* experience of those who visited the Globe and Fortune to see Shakespeare's plays. So, for example, in selecting illustrations of *memento mori*, I have resisted the temptation to focus on the magnificent fifteenth century dance of death series at the Church of St. Mary, Berlin, or the colorful Death pageant at Beram in Croatia. Instead, I look to the *danse macabre* at Boxgrove Priory, a short journey south from where the Globe Theatre stood; and to the extraordinary skeleton representations at St. Alban's Cathedral and at St. Andrew's Church, Oddington, both of which lie on the route from Stratford-on-Avon to London.

The method of this study, then, is to evaluate the correspondence between emblematic and iconic significances and textual and theatrical meaning. One danger of such an approach lies in the temptation to rely too heavily on iconographic evidence from the Medieval and Renaissance periods, supposing that Shakespeare's sources were entirely visual and that he neither read nor discussed nor listened. Most emblem books, combining word and picture, obviate this problem by virtue of their very format, and I have drawn extensively on the literal content of such works as well as their visual import. Funereal, church and cathedral art often carries with it extensive literary commentary, with inscriptions on stone or wood, and this, too, has informed the process of my analysis. In addition, I have relied heavily on non-emblematic textual sources to initiate or endorse parallels and to sustain the broader arguments of this book.

A further word of caution, though. Emblem books were a cross-European genre, and they achieved a high plateau of popularity that stretched from the mid-sixteenth century until late into the seventeenth. There was much that unified the emblematic literatures that traversed this broad historical and geographical sweep, and the sense of commonality was perhaps one of the singular achievements of the genre. Yet, there were also differences in quality and content. While, at their worst, emblem books were dull and imitative and moralistically tedious, at their best, they reflected extraordinary levels of artistic and poetic originality. It would be wrong, then, to think of all emblem books as formulaic and repetitious; and equally misguided to suppose that any one of them offers to the modern reader a set of standardized meanings that can be transposed, simply and accurately, from one time or place or text to another. Of course, this has the effect of rendering interpretations of a given emblem sometimes difficult, even slippery. I think, for example, of the Cupid and Death iconographic *topos* that forms an important part of discussion in Chapter 4. Here, in a succession of renditions that spanned a century, the emblems of Marquale, Lefèvre, Daza, Hunger, Whitney, and Peacham can all be traced to the genius of Andrea Alciati's *Emblematvm Libellvs* (1534). But although the debt to Alciati is clear and the similarities between prints obvious, almost every word and every line of the succeeding emblems speaks out against the charge of imitation. Inspirationally bonded to the master, each is yet masterly in its own way, demonstrating individualities of style and emphasis and detail.

Visual similarities between woodcuts, then, can be misleading, and we need to remember that iconographic analysis, generally, needs to be flexible and alert, aware that supposed connections are sometimes false and meanings occasionally contradictory. But while all these contingencies require us to be cautious and not over-bold in our readings, the emblems and allusions to them can be helpful. We know that the Elizabethans studied and loved them; there is reason to suspect, as well, that Shakespeare sometimes endorsed the conventional meanings of emblematic *topoi* and sometimes challenged them. These perceptions can only be given a measure of reliability with regard to the interpretation of a play if we consider a particular emblematic example within the wider ambit of its *topos*, defining its relationship to other instances of usage, and filtering the conventional from the unorthodox. This I have endeavored to do in *Emblems of Mortality*, drawing as widely and prudently as I can on iconographies that Shakespeare's generation would have known and understood (or thought they understood).

* * * * *

I have already mentioned some of the studies undertaken on the subject of death in the early modern period. Perhaps I may say a little now about work specifically on the emblem books. The importance of these texts to Renaissance literary studies was persuasively established in Rosemary Freeman's *English Emblem Books* (1948). Arthur Henkel and Albrecht Schöne's *Emblemata: Handbuch zur Sinnbildkunst des XVI. und XVII. Jahrhunderts* (1967) was the first major assemblage of Renaissance emblems. Shakespeare's knowledge of a deal of emblematic material was demonstrated in Henry Green's *Shakespeare and the Emblem Writers* (1964). These works provided Shakespeare scholars with an important emblematic repository. John Doebler's *Shakespeare's Speaking Pictures: Studies in Iconic Imagery* (1974)[2] offered a relatively early, and enduring, insight into the assimilation of picture and word but, on the whole, the study of the relationship between icon and text in Shakespeare's theatre did not develop rapidly. I find this curious because emblematic understanding was such an important dimension of sixteenth century social life. The great power of pictures is that you don't need to be literate to understand them. Shakespeare lived in an age where people had been conditioned to "read" pictures; or, as the Shakespearean phrase in Doebler's title would have it, the pictures "spoke" to the viewer. It is no accident that the names of theatres and ale houses and other public places in Shakespeare's day carried titles that were easily pictorialized: The Globe, The Swan, the Boar's Head Tavern, the Flying Horse Inn. The picture made the tavern or playhouse immediately recognizable and, for this very reason, civic officers took care to prevent duplication of names and signs in order to avoid confusion. The journeyman Ralph's mild perplexity about the sign of the Golden Ball and the sign of the Golden Shoe in Dekker's *The Shoemakers' Holiday* (IV.ii.112-21)[3] is a comic rendering of the age old problem of finding your away around unfamiliar places. In a time when most could not read, the average traveler relied more heavily on painted symbol than written word. He understood perfectly that pictures conveyed *meaning* as well as pleasure.

Two recent works have made notable progress in exploring the relationship between Shakespeare's theatre and, particularly, emblematic literatures. Kwang Soon Cho's *Emblems in Shakespeare's Last Plays* (1998) has affirmed the sophisticated significances that contemporary criticism is now able to articulate in relation to the emblem books and Shakespeare's plays. Cho explores how Shakespeare, using emblem and emblematic sources, constructs a moral and ethical framework in certain of his plays, and conveys this vision to his audience. In so doing, Cho relies successfully on the idea that there is a close paralleling between the emblem and the drama. Just as the emblem is composed of picture and poem, so, too, the theatre conflates visual spectacle with speech and gesture. The argument concludes, perhaps not surprisingly, that "A full understanding of the last plays as a whole is not possible without the knowledge of emblems in relation to their structure and morals."[4] It is worth noting, however, that some commentators (Daly[5], for example; but implicitly disputed by Freeman's definition[6] and Huston Diehl's endorsement[7] of it) have argued that emblematic literature does not necessarily make use of engravings. Andrew Willet's *Sacrorum Emblematum Centuria Una* (1592) is perhaps the most obvious example of an emblem book without pictures. In my own approach, I have assumed Daly's broader perspective.

Peggy Muñoz Simonds' *Myth, Emblem, and Music in Shakespeare's Cymbeline: An Iconographic Reconstruction* (1992) offers a scholarly exploration of icon and drama. A particular focus is the detail of Imogen's bedchamber, a room elaborately described in Shakespeare's text and one, as Simonds' study shows, loaded with embedded iconic significance. Simonds sees the decorative aspects of the bedroom as a reconciliation of opposites in which the iconography of primitive wild men is pitted satirically against the mores of English courtly life. She goes further to show how the iconographies of birds, animals, vegetation and minerals in *Cymbeline* establish clear resonances with the key themes of doubt, repentance, reformation, reunion and regeneration. The work makes considerable use of the emblem books but considers, as well, Renaissance embroidery, plaster work, paintings and sculpture — a valuable eclecticism, it seems to me, and an approach that I, too, have willingly embraced in *Emblems of Mortality*. I have no doubt that Shakespeare was well acquainted with a variety of emblem books, and I concur with Simonds that Geffrey Whitney's *A Choice a Emblemes* (1586) is foremost amongst these.[8] But the emblem books were not the only sources that could have inspired Shakespeare to reconstruct, and sometimes reinterpret, iconic motifs in his theatre. As I have noted already, the murals and mementos and funerary iconographies of churches and cathedrals, as well as the rich behest of illuminated manuscripts from earlier epochs, also provided popularly recognizable pictures of mortality.

Shakespearean scholarship has also been greatly assisted by recent emblematic publications not specifically related to Shakespeare. Peter Daly et al. have provided us with *The Latin Emblems* (1987) and *Emblems in Translation* (1988), two monumental tomes that document and cross-reference the work of Andrea Alciati, the best known of the sixteenth century emblematists, and those who drew inspiration from Alciati's work. Peter Daly, in fact, has been a notable champion of emblematic studies, working in collaboration with David Weston, Keeper of Special Collections at the University of Glasgow, and Scolar Press, to bring the genre to wider and more accessible scholarly attention. Charles Moseley has produced *A Century of Emblems* (1989), an important anthology of Renaissance emblems, presented with erudite commentary and interpretation. Michael Bath's *Speaking Pictures: English Emblem Books and Renaissance Culture* (1993) has rendered illuminating cultural insights; and Elizabeth Watson's *Bocchi and the Emblem Book As Symbolic Form* (1994) has afforded us an important and thoroughly researched study of a leading Italian emblematist. In addition, valuable reprints have been issued or reissued in recent years, most notably Claude Paradin's *Devises Heroiques* (1561; rpt. 1990), Geffrey Whitney's *A Choice of Emblemes* (1586; rpt. 1989), and Guillaume de la Perrière's *Le Theatre des bons engins* (1540; rpt. 1993). Jan Van der Noot's *A Theatre for Worldings* (1569; rpt. 1988) has appeared in *The English Emblem Tradition*, Vol. 1, ed. Peter Daly, with Leslie T. Duer and Anthony Raspa (Toronto: University of Toronto Press, 1988); and Thomas Combe's *The Theater of fine devices* (1593; rpt. 1993), a popular Elizabethan translation of la Perrière's masterpiece, was reprinted in the second volume of the Toronto series.

* * * * *

Emblems of Mortality is essentially an interdisciplinary investigation, embracing the visual arts, literature and religion. To disaggregate these, it seems to me, is to misunderstand one of the fundamental unities of the Renaissance. I have sought to achieve a solid referential base for each chapter, providing an exposition of the broader issues pertaining to a particular iconic *topos* before engaging in detailed studies of a play or plays relevant to it. This method, I hope, will render the book profitable not only to people interested in Renaissance drama but also to those who are working in other genres of Shakespeare's age or in periods adjacent to it. The manuscript combines literary criticism with careful scholarship; but it strives, above all, to be readable. My intention has been to provide a text that is, at once, challenging and stimulating for scholars of standing, and yet accessible and informative for college students setting out on serious Shakespearean studies.

Notes

1. Unless otherwise indicated, all references to Shakespeare's text are from G. Blakemore Evans et al., eds., *The Riverside Shakespeare*, 2nd Ed. (Boston: Houghton Mifflin, 1997).
2. John Doebler, *Shakespeare's Speaking Pictures: Studies in Iconic Imagery* (Albuquerque: University of New Mexico Press, 1974), pp. 21-38.
3. Thomas Dekker, *The Shoemakers' Holiday*, ed. D. J. Palmer, *Elizabethan and Jacobean Comedies: A New Mermaid Anthology*, introduced by Brian Gibbons (Tonbridge, Kent: Ernest Benn, 1984).
4. Kwang Soon Cho, *Emblems in Shakespeare's Last Plays* (Lanham: University Press of America, 1998), p. 139.
5. See the introduction (p. xi) to *The English Emblem Tradition*, Vol. 2, ed. Peter M. Daly, with Leslie T. Duer and Mary V. Silcox (Toronto: University of Toronto Press, 1993).
6. Rosemary Freeman, *English Emblem Books* (1948, first publ.; London: Chatto and Windus, 1967).
7. See the introduction to Huston Diehl's *English Emblem Books, 1500-1700* (Norman and London: University of Oklahoma Press, 1986), p. 4.
8. Peggy Muñoz Simonds, *Myth, Emblem, and Music in Shakespeare's Cymbeline: An Iconographic Reconstruction* (Newark: University of Delaware Press, 1992), notes that Whitney's work was "almost certainly known to Shakespeare" (p. 258).

Chapter 2

ℬℭℛℬ

Emblems of an English Eden

The sixteenth century made much of the idea of "life in death," one of its most popular visual metaphors being the phoenix, an exotic self-procreating bird which, as Pliny claimed, lived in Arabian spice trees.[1] Paradin's emblem in *Les Devises Heroiques* (1551) reveals the bird emerging from the ashes of its own fiery death.[2] Nicholas Reusner's *Emblemata Nicolai Revsneri* (1581), offering a similar image some thirty years later, summarizes a standard interpretation:

> If men report true, death over again forms the Phoenix,
> To this bird both life and death the same funeral pile may prove.
> Onward, executioners! Of the saints burn ye the sainted bodies;
> For whom ye desire perdition, to them brings the flame new birth.[3]

Reusner's meaning is unambiguously religious, drawing on the purgative qualities of fire which had been well rehearsed in the diktats emerging from the Roman Catholic Church's Council of Trent (1545-1563) and which, anyway, had been a commonplace since early Medieval times. The bird is less common in English church iconography, perhaps disadvantaged by its associations with Catholic notions of purgatory, an idea eschewed by Protestant England after the death of Queen Mary I in

1558. One example does exist in a misericord carving in Henry VII's Chapel at Westminster Abbey but it is conspicuous by its rarity.[4] Secular usage is more common. Geffrey Whitney, in *A Choice of Emblemes* (1586), imitates Paradin's print but avoids the overtly religious significances that both Paradin and Reusner accord to the icon.[5] For Whitney, the phoenix is a valuable image of secular resurrection, and his bird stands as a representation of the revivalist hopes of the town of Namptwiche in Cheshire which had been recently destroyed by a devastating fire. In sum, the phoenix suited well both religious and secular metaphors of regeneration, of life in death. Having spent its life, it disappeared in a fury of flames, only to rise again, alive and well, from its own ashes; an immortal bird, and yet also mortal.

A phoenix flutters irregularly through Shakespeare's early and middle canon.[6] It is a precocious (and secular) bird, appearing variously as a tavern in *The Comedy of Errors* (I.ii.75 etc.), a ship in *Twelfth Night* (V.i.61), an instrument of revenge in *1 Henry VI* (IV.vii.93), an expression of rarity in *As You Like It* (IV.iii.17), a variety of womanhood in *All's Well That Ends Well* (I.i.168), and the subject of narrative fable in *The Phoenix and Turtle*. The later work makes less of it, though there is one startling reference in *Henry VIII*, relating to the idea of monarchy regenerating itself from one reign to the next, and thereby defeating death through a perpetuating cycle of earthly glory. Baptizing the infant princess, Elizabeth, Archbishop Cranmer assures her father, Henry VIII, that

> as when
> The bird of wonder dies, the maiden phoenix,
> Her ashes new create another heir
> As great in admiration as herself,
> So shall she leave her blessedness to one
> When heaven shall call her from this cloud of darkness
> Who from the sacred ashes of her honor
> Shall star-like rise as great in fame as she was,
> And so stand fix'd. Peace, plenty, love, truth, terror,
> That were the servants to this chosen infant,
> Shall then be his, and like a vine grow to him.
> Where ever the bright sun of heaven shall shine,
> His honor and the greatness of his name
> Shall be, and make new nations.
>
> (*Henry VIII* V.iv.39-52)

If there was a greater concurrence of views that Shakespeare wrote *Henry VIII*, or if the play was simply more popular, Cranmer's comments might have ranked alongside Gaunt's English panegyric in *Richard II*. I say *might* because several facets of the speech serve to diminish its worth. First, there is the unashamed sycophantism which tends to jar on democratized ears. The infant Elizabeth had already reigned and died by the time Shakespeare (and whoever) came to write this play and her "heir," at whom all this prophesied glory is aimed, was James I — presently on the throne and patronizing theatre rather generously. Secondly, and more to our purposes here, the reference to the phoenix sits uncomfortably on the facts of the situation. True, it seems to express succinctly and admirably that paradox of regality, still uttered at the moment of succession to the English throne: "The king is dead. Long live the king!" The individual monarch may perish but the monarchy itself is immortal, perpetual, un-killable. But with regard to the actual circumstances to which Cranmer alludes (the succession of James I), the reverberations are somewhat implausible. No one could doubt the splendor of Elizabeth's reign but James had achieved little, save the accidental union of England and Scotland by dint of birth, and his penchant was not for chivalric and spiritual triumph but for reading and the occult.[7]

What Cranmer would really like to say, but can't, is that James is Elizabeth's son and familial inheritor, that her "Ashes new create[d] another heir," just as the infant Elizabeth was the inheritor of her biological father, Henry VIII, and just as the phoenix recreated itself from its own physical being. This would be to stretch reality further than even dramatic prerogative allows. The two monarchs were only distantly related: Elizabeth was a Protestant Tudor, James a Catholic Stuart. The point about the phoenix was that it was able to procreate the next physical version of itself, a lineal corollary that was pertinent to Henry VIII and Elizabeth but hardly applied to Elizabeth and James. On the contrary, the most compelling political issue in the years before the maiden queen's death was exactly that she had *not* produced a son and heir, and that, as a result, the door was being left frighteningly ajar for a Scottish Catholic to assume the throne of England.[8] The best the dramatist's hand could do was allow Cranmer deftly to fudge the issue, permitting him to infer likeness (not equation) through the "maiden phoenix" simile and confining him to the simple assertion that James would inherit Elizabeth's "blessedness" (line 43) and "honor" (line 45). But not her genes.

I want to move away from *Henry VIII's* vexatious phoenix and into the more pertinent domain inferred, but not articulated, in Cranmer's panegyric — namely, the sense of heroic *genetic* succession, the notion of direct familial inheritance, of the child inheriting from the parent. If Shakespeare and others wanted a better illustration of heroic familial inheritance, there were several examples available more persuasive than the Jacobite line.   Richard I, Coeur de lion, and his bastard son, Faulconbridge, for one; and Edward III and his son, the Black Prince, for another.   Shakespeare makes something of the Richard / Faulconbridge relationship in *King John*, offering in the form of Faulconbridge a super-hero who breaks the norms of devious bastardy and emerges as a potential kingly inheritor, albeit he never actually becomes king.   And though Coeur-de-Lion was admired by Tudor historians, most of his exploits were against the distant Arab infidel. By Elizabethan times the world of Arabia had become an alluringly exotic, rather than odious, landscape — a place of sweet perfumes (*Macbeth* V.i.50-1) and phoenixes (*The Tempest* III.iii.23-4).   There was little mileage in raking up an old and near-forgotten enemy when one had available, instead, the marvelous French-conquering chronicles of Edward III and the Black Prince. As military exemplars, the pair were unsurpassed in the Elizabethan imagination. Tudor historians lauded Edward III's exploits abroad with unfailing enthusiasm, ranging from John Rastell's populist *The Pastyme of the People*[9] to Caxton's weightier *Chronycles of Englande*.[10] A plethora of Elizabethan works on military prowess and skills made standard reference to Edward III as the primal illustration of the heroic militaristic traits they advocated — as in William Wyrley's *The Trve Vse of Armorie*[11] and Matthew Sutcliffe's *The Practice, Proceedings, And Lawes of armes*.[12]

The Black Prince was revered equally, with pen and brush stroke alike, in works as diverse as the *Mirror for Magistrates* (1555),[13] Raleigh's *Historie of the World* (1613),[14] and a late fifteenth century painting entitled "Adoration of the Magi" which portrays him as one of the three Magi.[15] The other two members of the triptych are Edward III and Richard II. So, in effect, we have a generational sequence visually represented, running from father to son to grandson. The religious import of the painting is edifying. By attaching to this family portrait the iconography of Biblical excellence, the artist at once reiterated the long-held idea of England as a blessed and sacred place, the "Fortunate Isles,"[16] but also suggested that the nature of the particular lineal inheritance was characterized by spiritual excellence. The Tudor chroniclers ignored the senility of Edward III, discreetly marginalized the unsavory reign of Richard, and clarioned the Black Prince as a peerless prince of chivalry — though, for those citizens of Limoges who suffered the barbarity of his Haute-Vienne reign of terror, peerless prince of chivalry may not have been the first phrase that jumped to mind. By the time the Edward / Black Prince chronicle reached the Elizabethan age, the formalin of time had solidified it into crystalline perfection, a pious artifact entirely impervious to sense or fact or reason.

Not surprisingly, in what was almost certainly the first history play he wrote, Shakespeare turns for early inspiration to the Edward III connection.

> Froissard, a countryman of ours, records
> England all Olivers and Rowlands bred
> During the time Edward the Third did reign.
> More truly now may this be verified,
> For none but Samsons and Goliases
> It sendeth forth to skirmish. One to ten!
> Lean raw-bon'd rascals! who would e'er suppose
> They had such courage and audacity?
>
> (Alençon, *1 Henry VI* I.ii.29-36)

Alençon's allusion is confused by the contradictory moral and social implications of a combination of French aristocratic heroes, English military legend, Biblical strongman, and gargantuan Philistine — none of which sits entirely comfortably with the image of scrawny, "raw-bon'd" Englishmen whose courage and audacity have inexplicably carried them to victory. No matter. The real issue for us here is that Alençon views English warriorship in *genetic* terms. The Englishmen who have that day defeated the French are the physical descendants of those magnificent combatants "bred" in the time of Edward III. Victory was in their DNA; it was something they inherited. In the same play, the image of the phoenix is deployed as a synonym for reviving English greatness. Lucy at first wishes "O, that I could but call these dead to life" (*1 Henry VI* IV.vii.81) and then threatens, of the English dead,

> from their ashes shall be rear'd
> A phoenix that shall make all France afeard.
>
> (IV.vii.92-3)

These new English terrors will be, we suppose, the next generation of "Olivers and Rolands" who were left in swaddling clothes when their fathers went off to fight and die in France.

James Calderwood has explored the interrelation of ideas of sexuality and death, arguing that to early modern European sensibilities "the human sexual act is never quite untinged with the shame of its animalistic associations."[17] This, he suggests, helps us to understand why it is that Shakespeare links immortality (derived from the cycle of procreation) with sexuality and death. Since sexual intercourse equates mankind with brute beasts, the erotic impulse derives not from God but from the apes.[18] Its source is therefore located in earthly physical transience rather than ethereal spiritual permanence. The challenge to Shakespeare's theatre, then, may be to build out of the baseness of the sexual act a cosmic scheme that brings a grandeur and dignity to the cycle of procreation and bestows upon it some form of "spiritualized" legitimacy. As we have seen already, the obligation of magnificent familial inheritance was an idea of some interest to Shakespeare in his treatment of the Henry VI era. He dwells on it elsewhere in the trilogy.

> O young John Talbot, I did send for thee
> To tutor thee in stratagems of war,
> That Talbot's name might be in thee reviv'd,
> When sapless age and weak unable limbs
> Should bring thy father to his drooping chair.
>> (Talbot to his son, *1 Henry VI* IV.v.1-5.)

> O brave young Prince! thy famous grandfather
> Doth live again in thee. Long mayst thou live
> To bear his image and renew his glories!
>> (Oxford to Edward, Prince of Wales,
>> *3 Henry VI* V.iv.52-4)

Talbot's name; in thee reviv'd; famous grandfather; live again in thee; bear his image; renew his glories. It was by no means unusual in Elizabethan theatre for those embarking on a military enterprise to invoke the names of their ancestors. Beaumont and Fletcher, in *The Knight of the Burning Pestle*, weave considerable burlesque out of Rafe's insistence on swearing "by the soule of *Amadis de Gaul*, / My famous Ancestor" (II.ii.55-6)[19] before setting out on his program of chivalric revenge. But the supplication to ancestry in Shakespeare's history plays takes the custom beyond the norm of casual allusion that characterizes it in Beaumont and Fletcher, and in the work of other Elizabethan and Jacobean dramatists, with the possible exception of Tourneur.

The great reputation of Talbot's "name" is documented by Edward Hall's *The Vnion of the two noble and illustre famelies of Lancastre & Yorke* (1548) which records that Talbot "obteined so many glorious victories of his enemies, that his only name was, and yet is dredful to the French."[20] Shakespeare's emphasis far exceeds the warrant of Hall's chronicle: at I.i.128 we are told that the English soldiers shouted "A Talbot! a Talbot!"; at I.iv.48-50 Talbot himself claims that the French so feared his name that they guarded him excessively; at II.i.79 an anonymous English soldier informs us that the cry of Talbot's name serves him as a sword; and John Talbot insists that he has a renowned name that must not be dishonored (IV.v.41). The importance that the dramatist places on Talbot's name as the by-word of a military mythology is paralleled by an insistence that Talbot's son, John, is not only the physical progeny of his father but his military heir as well. The hope that "Talbot's name might be in thee [John] reviv'd" underscores Shakespeare's mythologization of a process of physical and military regeneration of excellences. As far as it goes, the idea works effectively enough and we have a sense of an honorable entity passed down *familialy* from generation to generation. It is, though, a construct of only limited dimensions for its potential is stifled by historical fact. Talbot and his son are both dead by the end of *1 Henry VI* and, as far as they are concerned, the experiment with regenerating military excellences comes to an abrupt halt.

Oxford's expectations that Prince Edward will emulate the feats of his famous grandfather, Henry V, are similarly misplaced. The hope of heroic renewal is preempted by his protégé's early death, a possibility hinted at by the doomed youth himself: "And if I live until I be a man, / I'll win our ancient right in France again, / Or die a soldier as I liv'd a king" (*Richard III* III.i.91-3). His murder in the Tower of London, an act away, highlights Shakespeare's problem in attempting to reconstruct a line of familialy repeating greatness. There simply is no sustained scheme of splendidly regenerating mortality in the First Tetralogy — there is very little splendid mortality, *per se*. In an era scoured by civil war, the repetition of brutalities seems more indicative of the age than the revival of military excellences. Oxford's faith in the rebirth of famous conquering achievements in France, in the revival of glorious ancestral qualities, stands in the constant shadow of familial perversions. The instance, in II.v of *3 Henry VI*, where Father kills Son and laments, with an appropriate reproductive nuance, the cruelties "This deadly quarrel daily doth *beget!*" (II.v.88-91, emphasis added) is perhaps the most memorable of these.

The sense of moral distortion, of unwholesome regeneration, becomes associated, as well, with the figure of the phoenix. Having begun the tetralogy as Lucy's heroic image of English dead reviving to conquer the French (*1 Henry VI* IV.vii.92-3), the bird transposes itself into a specter of regenerating evil:

> My ashes, as the phoenix, may bring forth
> A bird that will revenge upon you all;
> And in that hope I throw mine eyes to heaven,
> Scorning what e'er you can afflict me with.
> > (York to his English foes, *3 Henry VI* I.iv.35-8)

> *Q. Elizabeth.* Yet thou didst kill my children.
> *K. Richard.* But in your daughter's womb I bury them;
> Where in that nest of spicery, they will breed
> Selves of themselves, to your recomforture.
> > (*Richard III* IV.iv.422-5)

The first of these is excerpted from the tormenting of York in I.iv of *3 Henry VI*, and presents Englishman pitted against Englishmen. In the previous scene young Rutland, Henry's son, had been slain by Clifford, despite his protestations that he had never done his murderer any harm. "Thy father slew my father; therefore die," says Clifford as he stabs the boy at I.iii.47. The recycling of evils becomes inextricably intertwined with the notion of physical regeneration from parent to offspring. The idea of evil procreated from generation to generation was one developed in the later Jacobean theatre, notably in *The Changeling* and *The White Devil*.[21] There, though, it served to express the pervasive malignity of a shadowy Mediterranean world that, like no other, at once fascinated and repelled Jacobean sensibilities. For *Henry VI*'s first audiences the crudities of English civil war were frighteningly proximate. The Battle of Bosworth Field (1485), the last great battle of the Wars of the Roses, bringing to an end a calamitous century of civil strife, would have been within living memory for a scattering of the early Elizabethans. It was that close. In such a savage period of English history, Rutland's murder was not exceptional in its brutality. Nor even, perhaps, was that of his father, York, killed in the very next scene of *3 Henry VI*. After being taunted with a handkerchief dipped in the blood of his beloved Rutland, and having been compelled to wear a paper crown, York is ritually slain. The phoenix that he wishes upon his foes turns out to be his son Richard, later King Richard III — he, in fact, who invokes the next phoenix image of the tetralogy. His is a bizarre and obscene restatement of the regenerative life-in-death theme. Having murdered one set of children, his metaphor promises to breed new children from the dead, to conjure them to life in Margaret's nest of spicery. It is ostensibly a gesture of atonement but actually yet another endeavor to find gratification in physical or manipulative cruelty. Even so, its infernal logic somehow persuades Elizabeth and she rushes off immediately to sway her daughter to the enterprise.

It is hard for me to imagine how Elizabeth could be taken in so by this charlatan. That may be because, as people claim, he was magnetically charismatic; or it could be because the phoenix doesn't loom large in my life, but for Elizabeth it signaled a compelling association. Its regenerating peculiarities were linked in sixteenth century mythography with the sacking and burning of Troy and, by implication, with the rise, from its ashes, of the great states of Europe. As most English people born before 1700 knew, England, too, was founded by a Trojan — the worthy Brutus, from whose name the term "Britain" derived. We live in "another Troy" says Gloucester in *3 Henry VI* III.ii.190 and, as if in evidence, the First Tetralogy positively groans with Classical allusion. Every significant figure of the Trojan siege, mortal or immortal, Greek or Trojan, is there: Helen, Menelaus, Agamemnon, Paris, Hector, Anchises, Aeneas, Hercules, Nestor, Ulysses, Venus, Mars, Priam, Achilles, Ajax, Diomedes. The pageant seems unending and Shakespeare fails to harness and manage it effectively. There is certainly a semblance of Virgilian or Homeric myth in the *Henry VI* plays, of an attempt to harmonize with the ancient epic resonances, but the inconsistencies of detail and development allow us to speak with assurance of only the feel of the Troy saga. The sense of momentous catastrophe seems unconvincing in Shakespeare's chronicle. With the fall of the civilization of Troy came to an end a golden age of arts and science, of soldiership and chivalry, of beauty and love. The very core of what we might call humanism. A legend was destroyed; but it was resurrected, phoenix-like, by the exceptional

individuals who emerged from its flames and lived to shape the mortal
world again. To compare Henry's England to Priam's Troy is to compare
the sinking of a river barge to that of the Titanic — equally tragic for the
victims, without doubt, but lacking the romantic pathos that history is
apt to bestow upon exceptional loss.

What seems absent from the First Tetralogy is the presence of anyone,
or any process, that can regenerate some kind of English heroic myth.
Without this, the phoenix metaphors and the Dardanian parallels echo
dissonantly and even grotesquely. Here, for example, young Clifford, is
bearing the body of his father in *2 Henry VI* and talking like a Trojan:

> In cruelty will I seek out my fame.
> [*He takes him up on his back.*]
> Come, thou new ruin of old Clifford's house:
> As did Aeneas old Anchises bear,
> So bear I thee upon my manly shoulders. . . .
>   (V.ii.60-3)

A popular woodcut of Shakespeare's age shows Aeneas carrying his
living father on his shoulders, while Troy burns in the background.[22]
The episode was held as a consummate illustration of filial duty by
European emblematists. Alciati's woodcut archetype of the incident was
copied by Lefèvre, Marquale, Daza, and Hunger,[23] and reproduced by
Geffrey Whitney in *A Choice of Emblemes* (*plate 5*).[24] At a superficial
level, the theatrical emblem Young Clifford presents is reminiscent of
the classical archetype, and no one can doubt his filial loyalty. But the
referential harmonies are all awry. Alciati's verse adage, and Whitney's
gloss of it, both emphasize that Aeneas' greatest glory was in *saving* his
father. In *2 Henry VI*, there is no rescue, merely a retrieval. In fact,
Clifford does not carry his father "As did Aeneas old Anchises bear,"
for the father he carries on his shoulders is dead; and his vow to seek out
fame "In cruelty" is most un-Trojan in demeanor.

Young Clifford's action summarizes the paradox that "Sex is life but
also death,"[25] to use Calderwood's words. The human ability to procreate
derives explicitly from the transgression in the garden of Eden, a
transgression that brought about the certainty of death. Humans, like
other "ordinary" creatures, must endure the same cycle of life and death.
The distinguishing factor, in Shakespeare's vision of splendid England,
is the chivalric spirit of earthly magnificence which lends to the animalistic

procreative process a sense of worth and grandeur. Young Clifford's willingness to deplete the myth, by promising cruelty instead of chivalric excellence, attests to a reversion to animalism — and to a state where human beings are indistinguishable from brute beasts. His invocation of the familiar Trojan icon, of son carrying father, mirrors the visual import of Alciati's print but carries a very different meaning.

* * * * *

The suggestion of a reviving Trojan paradise in the Yorkist cycle is both weak and distorted. All was not lost, though. The brief flurry of English history from the deposition of Richard II (1399) to Henry V's miraculous triumph at Agincourt (1415) provided Shakespeare with material more amenable to his heroic English designs than the grim, grinding reign of Henry VI had done. Here, the enfeebled and seedy kingship of Richard would be brought to an end by the dashing Bullingbrook (a name refashioned as "Bolingbroke"[26] in the eighteenth century). And, in turn, his son, King Henry V, would carry English aspirations to unimaginable heights in France. Enlightened and perhaps chastened by the experiences of the First Tetralogy, Shakespeare set about the construction of a new English paradisial myth, one founded upon a principle of life-in-death, of heroic genetic inheritance. I have used the word "paradisial" deliberately here. Gaunt's reference to "This other Eden, demi-paradise" (II.i.42) in *Richard II* is well known, but Shakespeare was far from original in framing England in such terms.[27] More, Sylvester, Lightfoot, and Greene had all recounted the idea of an English Eden before Shakespeare wrote *Richard II*.[28] The term "paradise," generally, was one the Elizabethans and Jacobeans bandied about liberally, and not only with reference to England. Thomas Stocker (1583) refers to the Low Countries as "the Paragone, or rather, yearthly Paradise, of all the Countries in Europe."[29] To Captain Bingham (1583), Newfoundland is "The paradise, of all the world."[30] And Silvester Jourdan (1613) calls Bermuda "one of the sweetest Paradises that be vpon the earth."[31] There was, though, a special affection for the idea of England as the ancient location of paradise and Elizabethan cartographers bent their compasses backwards trying to prove the matter scientifically.

If Gaunt's England is a paradise, an "other Eden," in what sense is it or was it or could it be paradisial? In the original Garden of Eden there was physical immortality. Adam and Eve would never die, just as long as they didn't succumb to the temptations of the fruit of the Tree of Knowledge. Succumb they did. God's punishment was expulsion from Eden and the revocation of their immortality (Genesis 3:17-18). Henceforth, they would grow old and physically die. In the Biblical paradigm, life-in-death meant spiritual life following physical death, a meaning commonly understood in both secular and religious literature. Baldock, in Marlowe's *Edward II*, for example, urges the younger Spenser to "Make for a new life, man; throw up thy eyes / And heart and hand to heaven's immortal throne" (IV.vi.107-8).[32] On this literal level of immortality, Gaunt's Eden in *Richard II* is quite different to the Biblical Eden and to Baldock's vision of unearthly paradise — but then, Gaunt is very careful to make the distinction. England is not Eden but a "second" Eden, a "demi" (= second) paradise. It is paradisial in a uniquely English way. Consider the expanded context of Gaunt's claim:

> This royal throne of kings, this scepter'd isle,
> This earth of majesty, this seat of Mars,
> This other Eden, demi-paradise,
> This fortress built by nature for herself
> Against infection and the hand of war,
> This happy breed of men, this little world,
> This precious stone set in the silver sea,
> Which serves it in the office of a wall,
> Or as a moat defensive to a house,
> Against the envy of less happier lands,
> This blessed plot, this earth, this realm, this England,
> This nurse, this teeming womb of royal kings,
> Fear'd by their breed, and famous by their birth,
> Renowned for their deeds as far from home,
> For Christian service and true chivalry,
> As is the sepulchre in stubborn Jewry
> Of the world's ransom, blessed Mary's Son
> (*Richard II* II.i.40-56)

There is a reasonably cogent explanation here of what an English paradise *is*. Those, like Willy Maley, who have argued so passionately for a declamation of this speech as serving "imperialist rhetoric"[33] are really stating no more than the obvious. The Elizabethans saw absolutely nothing wrong with being imperialists, as the writings of any number of super-opinionated propagandists of the age affirm. Gaunt's definition of the anglicized Eden, deriving from widely and strongly held views on the notion of "paradise," is partially "static" and partially "active." The stasis of paradise consists of that which is given, fixed and immovable. The fact that England is the "seat of Mars" is irrevocable. A tradition of Mars as the patron-god of England had been extant since the Middle Ages. It is also a holy land, a "blessed" plot favored by God and renowned for its Christian service. These, too, in the Elizabethan psyche, were immutable truisms, historical facts that could not be obliterated or lost.

Though Gaunt's second Eden offers that which is fixed and immovable, it remains merely a latent paradise unless those who live in the present can enliven it, refurbish it, build upon it. This, too, is clear from Gaunt's prescription. England may be a fortress built against "infection and the hand of war" and its surrounding sea may act as a "moat defensive" but fortresses can be assailed and moats breached. The active duty of those who inhabit paradise is to preserve its paradisial characteristics from inward strife and outward invasion. Equally, the English Eden may have nurtured many a great king, who performed many a mighty act, but unless that kind of regenerating splendor can be actively maintained, the demi-paradise stands simply as a memory, a thing of recollection rather than contemporary experience. The myth of an English paradise, then, consists of that which is immovable and of that which must be given "new life." For Gaunt, England under the rule of Richard is now no more than a shadow of its former greatness. It has become a landscape of death and despair and stagnation.

Things change quickly. Within a few hundred lines of Gaunt's English panegyric and his ensuing lament, a cadre of disaffected nobleman is lamenting the fate of an England ruled by Richard and deprived of Bullingbrook. One suggests that their future suffering is now unavoidable. Another disagrees:

> Not so, even through the hollow eyes of death
> I spy life peering, but I dare not say
> How near the tidings of our comfort is.
> (II.i.270-2)

Northumberland is understandably shifty here. The "life peering," to which he alludes, is none other than Harry Hereford who has decided to un-banish himself and make his way back to England with eight ships and three thousand fully armed militiamen. Northumberland's cryptic

clue heralds his return. It was also Northumberland who brought news
of Gaunt's death, just over a hundred lines earlier (II.i.147-51). So here
is a man well positioned to compass the life and death of Lancastrian
inheritance. There is no phoenix allusion here, but the idea of "life-in-
death" appeared in many forms. For example, the seventeenth print in
Hans Holbein's *Icones Historiarvm Veteris Testamenti* shows Adam and
Eve after their expulsion from Eden (*plate 6*).[34] Adam is clearing a root
from a bare stretch of earth. He is assisted, almost shadowed, by a
skeletal Death figure. In the background, Eve nurses her first-born son.
Once expelled from paradise, Adam and Eve become subject to the familiar
mortal cycle of life and death. That is what the skeleton signifies. Yet,
this is no disdainful, scorning skeleton. Here is a skeleton with a solid
work ethic, for in levering the root with Adam he does his best to assist
in the cultivation of this bleak landscape. So, the world of fallen Adam
is not entirely without consolation. Even as he labors in the certainty of
eventual death, his child lies in the arms of mother Eve. There is the
actuality of physical generation, of new hope, of a life not without purpose,
symbolically portrayed by Holbein through the suggestion and promise
of sown seed and the smile on Eve's lips. Yes, Adam and Eve will die;
but they will live too. Death is an important mechanism in the cycle of
regenerating life. Just as Adam and his skeletal friend extricate old roots
from stony ground, so, eventually, new roots will flourish until they,
too, are swept away in the inexorable march of time. In this unending
round of life, perpetuation relies on the principle of inheritance, on a
generation fulfilling its rôle to that which will succeed it, rejoicing in
what is to come and exulting in what has been.

Holbein's *Icones* was one of the most successful of all sixteenth
century emblem books, an English version appearing within two years of
its first publication. The artist himself was particularly popular in England,
and a favorite at the court of Henry VIII. Even if Shakespeare had not
known the detail of this print, there are any number of other life-in-death
sources in the emblem books which would have made the point, and less
obliquely too. In the Antwerp issue of *Emblemata* (1564), Joannes
Sambucus offers, as his final device, a plant flourishing out of the top of
a skull.[35] Claude Paradin, in *Les Devises Heroiques* (1551), translated
into English as *The Heroicall Devises* in 1591, depicts sprigs of wheat
growing from bones and adds the motto "Spes altera vitae" which may
be rendered as either "Another hope of life" or "The hope of another
life" (*plate 7*).[36] Joachim Camerarius, in 1595, repeats Paradin's emblem

and uses the same ambiguous Latin adage.[37] Some forty years later, George Wither published *A Collection of Emblemes* (largely an assemblage of prints from earlier periods) and chose as his twenty-first emblem a skull with sprigs of wheat growing out of the eyes and mouth (*plate 8*):

> When we are Borne, to Death-ward straight we runne;
> And by our Death, our Life is new-begunne.[38]

This couplet provides a fitting conclusion to Wither's commentary on what is, in essence, an image of wholesome life peering through the hollow eyes of death.

One central idea emerges from the life-in-death iconography of Wither, Holbein and the other emblematists I have mentioned. The intentions of each icon are specifically religious, promoting the meaning that physical death leads to spiritual life in heaven — an idea that John Donne expanded in his celebrated "Death's Duel" sermon, subtitled "the dying Life and living Death of the Body."[39] Even as the emblematists propagated this message of spiritual resurrection, they were doing so through highly physicalized motifs. Wither's notion of "Life . . . new-begunne" is conveyed through the tangible representation of a living, growing plant; Sambucus, and Paradin do likewise. And, of course, Holbein's picture of smiling Eve with "Life . . . new-begunne" in her arms is almost heretical in its humanism. It is a short step from these ideas to the sense of new life as physical procreation, a notion aptly articulated by Audley in *Edward III*, a play, as Tobin[40] has noted, in which Shakespeare's hand is quite possibly present:

> For from the instant we begin to live
> We do pursue and hunt the time to die:
> First bud we, then we blow, and after seed;
> Then presently we fall, and as a shade
> Follows the body, so we follow death.
>   (*Edward III* IV.iv.136-40)[41]

Audley's sense is rather more reflective than triumphalist, but two of the central motifs of the emblem books are present: the image of vegetation and the cyclical notion of seeding and death. What is absent here, but attendant elsewhere in the play, is the sense of inherited chivalric spirit, of son replicating father in an unending cycle of English greatness.

Northumberland's speculation in *Richard II* that "even through the hollow eyes of death / I spy life peering" has, then, both a physical and a spiritual sense. Harry Hereford is the flesh and blood son of his father. More than that, Northumberland understands him to be, as well, the spiritual descendant of his father. The iconographical incompatibility of physical life and spiritual life is here abandoned. In the dramatist's view of regenerating English excellence on earth, the two become mutually dependent. Notice how earlier in the play Hereford had addressed his father as he prepared for battle with Mowbray:

> O thou, *the earthly author of my blood*,
> Whose *youthful spirit, in me regenerate*,
> Doth with a twofold vigor lift me up
> To reach at victory above my head,
> Add proof unto mine armor with thy prayers,
> And with thy blessings steel my lance's point,
> That it may enter Mowbray's waxen coat
> And *furbish new the name* of John a' Gaunt,
> Even in the lusty havior of his son.
>
> (I.iii.69-77, emphasis added)

This is exactly what Canterbury and Ely tell Bullingbrook's son in *Henry V* when he is about to set out in chase of the French crown. Well, not quite exactly, because there no one mentions his father, Bullingbrook, or his grandfather Gaunt. The focus is on the unequivocal legitimacy of his great-great-grandfather, Edward III, and of his great-uncle, the Black Prince. Here, Hereford thinks along immediate familial lines, proposing a simple paradigm of a son inheriting, and living up to, the name of his father. It is quintessentially a humanist ambition. Gaunt is the "earthly author" of his blood but the "youthful spirit" of which he talks in line 70, and the "prayers" and "blessings" in the three lines that follow, endow this earthly enterprise with its own kind of "secular" sanctity. This explains why there is no mention of God, and still an unmistakable sense of heroic "spirituality" in his words. Gaunt offers something similar when he talks of England as "This land of such dear souls, this dear, dear land, / Dear for her reputation through the world" (*Richard II* II.i.57-8). The "souls" are dear not for their piety but for their earthly "reputation." While the Biblical ideal of life-in-death offers a clear disjunction between the flesh and the soul, the conception of Gaunt and

Hereford harmonizes them, attaching to the ideas of soul or spirit that sense of intangible *earthly* honor.[42]

Shakespeare's designs in his early historical works reveal a willingness to manipulate life-in-death imagery experimentally. Images of heroic renewal are subverted into representations of cyclical depravity; the process of inheritance, as a defeat of mortal death, is reconstructed as a bequest of death. This is understandable in situations of moral ambiguity, and these were plentiful in those reigns that preceded and followed the golden age of Henry V. The construction of an English Eden, foreshadowed by the Trojan innuendoes of the First Tetralogy and Gaunt's paradisial vision, and founded on the notion of regenerating humanity and warlike spirit, would seem to find its natural domain in the French exploits of Henry V. In fact, if this was Shakespeare's intention, it falls short of the mark as many have observed. Patricia Carlin, for example, suggests that the defiance of death, having failed in the preceding histories, is again engaged within the particular circumstances of *Henry V*.[43] But she notices, also, that "The king who presides over this play is a figure new to drama, a ruler who is associated with life and death at the same time" (p. 89). Marlovians may contest the claim to uniqueness but it is certainly true that Shakespeare's Henry is, at once, the ultimate hero of English myth and yet persistently linked with what Carlin calls "the infliction of death" (p. 89).

Disturbing as this overview may be, the opening of *Henry V* reveals few signs of ambivalence. This is not surprising for a play that sets out to portray the most illustrious epoch of French-bashing since Poitiers. And perhaps small wonder, too, that it is to Edward III and his son, the Black Prince, that Shakespeare quickly returns. Near the outset of *Henry V*, and after Canterbury has completed his lengthy genealogical exposition in support of Henry's proposed expedition to capture the French crown, the king asks obtusely: "May I with right and conscience make this claim?" (I.ii.96) — and this after the Archbishop has just spent sixty-three lines endeavoring to answer the same. Immediately, Canterbury and Ely all but abandon the Salic argument and, enjoined by Exeter, appeal instead to a second source of moral justification:

> *Canterbury.* Gracious lord,
> Stand for your own, unwind your bloody flag,
> *Look back into your mighty ancestors*;
> Go, my dread lord, to your great-grandsire's [Edward III's] tomb,

> From whom you claim; *invoke his warlike spirit,*
> And your great-uncle's, Edward the Black Prince,
> Who on the French ground play'd a tragedy,
> Making defeat on the full power of France,
> Whiles his most mighty father on a hill
> Stood smiling to behold his lion's whelp
> Forage in blood of French nobility.
> O noble English, that could entertain
> With half their forces the full pride of France,
> And let another half stand laughing by,
> All out of work and cold for action!
>   *Ely.* *Awake remembrance of these valiant dead,*
> And with your puissant arm *renew their feats.*
> *You are their heir*, you sit upon their throne;
> The blood and courage that renowned them
> *Runs in your veins*; and my thrice-puissant liege
> Is in the very May-morn of his youth,
> Ripe for exploits and mighty enterprises.
>   *Exeter.* Your brother kings and monarchs of the earth
> Do all expect that you should *rouse yourself,*
> *As did the former lions of your blood.*
>   (I.ii.100-24, emphasis added)

Canterbury takes us back to Henry's "great-grandsire's tomb"; Ely speaks of "these valiant dead"; and Exeter remembers Edward III and the Black Prince as "former lions of your blood." Balanced against this emphasis on physical mortality is the powerful notion of regeneration. The word "spirit," with its Hebraic overtones, is here anglicized into a mythology of heroic earthly renewal. It becomes a metaphor for a fine quality of military conduct and competence that can and ought to be passed on from one generation to the next. The "warlike spirit" of Edward III and the Black Prince stands outside the domain of physical mortality, never irretrievably lost in the death of the individual but, paradoxically, relying for perpetuation on the spawning of heirs. King Henry is not simply the physical descendant of his great ancestors, but their "spiritual" inheritor as well. The Archbishop insists that he must stand for his own and "Look back into your mighty ancestors" for, in aspiring to their "warlike spirit," he may awake remembrance of them and, with his puissant arm, "renew their feats."

The "renewal" of heroic royalty, of the warlike kingly spirit, parallels the physical "renewal" of the progenitor in the lives of his offspring. The relation of Edward III to his great son the Black Prince is the best possible exemplification of this — and Henry V is of their lineage. "You are their heir; you sit upon their throne," the Bishop of Ely tells the king, and adds: "The blood and courage that renowned them / Runs in your veins." It is this peculiar mix of "blood and courage," as Ely puts it, of the physical and the abstract, that defines the nature of regal English inheritance. Henry does not stand in isolation. His debt to the past and, particularly, to the English ideal, is profound and unavoidable. Those, his ancestors, who have afforded him earthly life, he must reciprocate with heroic spiritual renewal. In fact, the Duke of Exeter, adding his testimony to the strength of the argument, observes that Henry's brother kings and monarchs "*expect* that you should rouse yourself, / As did the former lions of your blood" (emphasis added). This statement of open "expectation," following hard upon the string of imperatives that Canterbury and Ely have leveled at the king, proposes the emulation of past heroic deeds as a kind of moral obligation. The genuine resurrection of an ancient kingly spirit becomes a moral necessity. In effect, it represents the demand, already discussed in relation to *Richard II*, to turn the latency of an English paradise into a kinetic, living actuality.

As I have suggested implicitly already, Shakespeare didn't suddenly arrive at this notion of regenerating English greatness in *Henry V* in a moment of arcane inspiration. He had been experimenting with the idea for perhaps ten years, his subject matter being the four plays of the First Tetralogy, and the first three of the Second. In these earlier plays, regeneration is presented in various forms — clumsily at first, but with a growing sense of assurance and artistry. By *Richard II* and the *Henry IV* his power is altogether more focused. Gone are the promiscuities of allusion and the inconsistent paralleling. In their place is a concerted and coherent attempt to articulate schemata of inheritance. I say schemata because there is more than one scheme. There is the benign sense of glorious regeneration, of a sort we have encountered already in *Henry V* and which finds expression, too, in *Richard II*. It is shadowed, though, by the deposition and murder of Richard II, a crime, as Michael Neill has suggested, that complicates and intensifies Bullingbrook's desire for retribution with "a profound nostalgia for a vanished prelapsarian order."[44] The English paradise may be as readily lost as its biblical equivalent, and the landscape of beauties transformed into a blasted and death-blighted plain.   To this theme is linked a different and grotesque life-in-death regeneration — a process of cyclical monstrosity which runs parallel to the idea of heroic inheritance and which is discernible in the early works but most cogently developed in *Henry IV*.

Notes

1. Pliny (Plinius Secundus), *The Secrets and wonders of the worlde. A booke ryght rare and straunge, contayning many excellent properties, giuen to Man, Beastes, Foules, fishes, and Serpents, Trees and Plants* (London: T. Hacket, 1587), Eiii, p. 4. The book is an abstract translation (possibly by Hacket).

2. It also appears in the Elizabethan translation of the work. Paradin, *The Heroicall Devises* (London: William Kearney, 1591), trans. P. S., p. 110.

3. Nicholas Reusner, *Emblemata Nicolai Revsneri* (Frankfurt: 1581), p. 98.

4. M. D. Anderson, in *History and Imagery in British Churches* (London: John Murray, 1995), p. 249, suggests that this is the only known example of a phoenix in an English holy place — though it is possible that the many instances of birds with strangely branching tails may have been intended to represent phoenixes.

5. Geffrey Whitney, *A Choice of Emblemes* (Leyden: Christopher Plantin, 1586), p. 177. Whitney's final emblem (p. 230) conjoins the idea of the "Phoenix rare" which "in time her selfe doth burne" with a final salutation to his queen and country.

6. For a discussion of the phoenix and its particular relation to Imogen in *Cymbeline*, see Peggy Muñoz Simonds, *Myth, Emblem, and Music in Shakespeare's Cymbeline: An Iconographic Reconstruction* (Newark: University of Delaware Press, 1992), pp. 228-37.

7. It seems to have been a wishful fashion of the age, though, to imagine King James as some kind of conquering colossus. Joshua Sylvester calls him implausibly "un Charle-magne encore" in his translation *Du Bartas. His Diuine Weekes and Workes with A Compleate Collectio of all the other most delight-full Workes* (London: 1605), sig. A2v; and Daniel Price (1613) is only marginally more judicious in styling James' son as "The Hope of Svcession, Englands Charlemaine" in *Lamentations for the death of the late Illustrious Prince Henry: and the dissolution of his religious Familie* (London: Tho. Snodham for R. Jackson, 1613), dedication leaf.

8. The religious inferences of the play have been much discussed. For example, Lee Bliss in "The Wheel of Fortune and the Maiden Phoenix of Shakespeare's King Henry the Eighth," *ELH*, 42 (1975), notes what he describes as "the dubious view that *Henry VIII* focuses on the defeat of Catholicism and the rise of Protestantism" (10).

9. John Rastell, *The Pastyme of the People The Chronycles of dyuers realmys and most specyally of the realme of England* (London: 1529), sigs. C5r-D3r.

10. William Caxton, *Chronycles of Englande* (St. Albans: 1483).

11. William Wyrley, *The Trve Vse of Armorie, Shewed by Historie, and plainly proued by example* (London: J. Jackson for Gabriell Cawood, 1592), p. 81: "Princely *Edward* mirror of Cheualrie."

12. Matthew Sutcliffe, *The Practice, Proceedings, And Lawes of armes, described out of the doings of most valiant and expert Captaines, and confirmed both by ancient, and moderne examples, and praecedents* (London: Christopher Barker, 1593), sig. B3r.

13. *The Mirror for Magistrates*, ed. Lily B. Campbell (New York: Barnes & Noble Inc., 1960), p. 93. The *Mirror* is believed to have been first published in 1555.

14. Sir Walter Raleigh, *Selections from his Writings*, ed. G.E. Hadow (Oxford: The Clarendon Press, 1917), pp. 93-4. Raleigh cites the Black Prince as an example of the supremacy of the English soldier in foreign battle.

15. The print is housed in the Warburg Institute, London, and is titled "Adoration of the Magi." It presents Edward III (father), Edward the Black Prince (son), and Richard II (grandson) as the three Magi.

16. Josephine Waters Bennett has explored the notion of England as "Elizium" citing, as one of her examples, Procopius of Caesarea who recounts a third-century legend that the souls of the dead were ferried across the English Channel to Britain. See "Britain Among The Fortunate Isles," *Studies in Philology*, 53 (1956), p. 123.

17. James L. Calderwood, *Shakespeare and the Denial of Death* (Amherst: University of Massachusetts Press, 1987), p. 49.

18. Calderwood, p. 50.

19. Francis Beaumont, *The Knight of the Burning Pestle*, ed. Andrew Gurr (Berkeley and Los Angeles: The University of California Press, 1966).

20. Edward Hall, in the opening paragraph of *The Vnion of the two noble and illustre fameliez of Lancastre & Yorke* (London: Richard Grafton, 1584), fol. 1.

21. In Thomas Middleton and William Rowley's *The Changeling*, ed. N. W. Bawcutt (Manchester: Manchester University Press, 1994), Beatrice grieves that "Vengeance begins; / Murder, I see, is followed by more sins. / Was my creation in the womb so curs'd, / It must engender with a viper first?" (III.iv.163-6). And Vittoria in John Webster's *The White Devil*, ed. John Russell Brown (Manchester: Manchester University Press, 1992), surmises her own tragedy in similar terms: "O my greatest sin lay in my blood. / Now my blood pays for't" (V.vi.240-1).

22. Andrea Alciati, *Emblemata* (Padua: Tozzi, 1621), emblem 195. This is an assemblage of Latin prints originally published in the period 1534-1551.

23. Jehan Lefèvre, *Emblèmes* (Paris: Wechel, 1536), emblem 69; Giovanni Marquale, *Imprese* (Lyon: Bonhomme, 1551), emblem 168; Bernardino Daza, *Emblemas* (Lyon: Bonhomme, 1549), emblem 69; Wolfgang Hunger, *Emblemata* (Paris: Wechel, 1542), emblem 69.

24. Whitney, p. 163.
25. Calderwood, p. 55.
26. As noted in a footnote to the Introduction, this book uses *The Riverside Shakespeare*, 2nd Ed., eds. G. Blakemore Evans et al. (Boston: Houghton Mifflin, 1997) as the standard text of Shakespeare's works. Following the *Riverside* edition, I have preserved the name "Bullingbrook" (as opposed to the modernized "Bolingbroke") since this is the form used in the earliest texts of *Richard II* and also in Holinshed, though sometimes without the "g." The form "Bolingbroke" is an early eighteenth century invention, attributed to Alexander Pope. I should add that on other occasions I have had cause to dispute the *Riverside*'s textual editing, but in this instance, at least, the case it makes for "Bullingbrook" (p. 847) seems reasonable.
27. See, for example, Clayton G. MacKenzie, "Paradise and Paradise Lost in *Richard II*," *Shakespeare Quarterly*, 37 (1986), pp. 318-39.
28. Edward Surtz, ed., *Utopia* (New Haven: Yale University Press, 1964), p. 59n, quotes Erasmus as saying that More's *Utopia* "represented chiefly Britain" (*Ep.* 4.21). See also Joshua Sylvester, p. 462: "All Haile (deere Albion) Europes Pearle of price, / The worlds rich Garden, Earths rare Paradice."
29. Thomas Stocker in the "Epistle Dedicatorie" to his translation of Marnix van Sant Aldegonde's *A Tragicall Historie of the troubles and Ciuile Warres of the lowe Countries, otherwise called Flanders* (London: 1583), sig. A2r.
30. The line is found in Bingham's prefatory poem to G. Peckham's *A Trve Report, Of the late discoueries, and possession, taken in the right of the Crowne of Englande, of the New-found Landes* (London: 1583), p. 10.
31. The quotation is from "The Epistle Dedicatorie" to Silvester Jourdan's *A Plaine Description of the Barmvdas, now called Sommer Ilands* (London: 1613), sig. A3r.
32. Christopher Marlowe, *The Complete Plays*, ed. J. B. Steane (Harmondsworth: Penguin Books, 1973).
33. Willy Maley, "'This sceptred isle': Shakespeare and the British problem" in *Shakespeare and National Culture*, ed. John J. Joughin (Manchester and New York: Manchester University Press, 1997), p. 94. Maley's chapter (pp. 83-108) provides a witty and erudite declamation of the English assumptions of Shakespeare's theatre.
34. Hans Holbein, *Icones Historiarvm Veteris Testamenti* (Lvgdvni: apud Ioannem Frellonium, 1547), sig. B1v. *Icones Historiarvm Veteris Testamenti* (1547) was translated into English within two years and appeared in various languages across Europe in the decades that followed. See Arthur B. Chamberlain, *Hans Holbein The Younger* (London: George Allen, 1913), II, p. 186.

35. Joannes Sambucus, *Emblemata, cum aliquot nummis antiqui operis, Ioannis Sambuci Tirnaviensis Pannonii* (Antwerp: 1564), p. 240.

36. Claude Paradin, *Les Devises Heroiques* (1551 first publ.; Anvers: 1561), p. 151r.

37. The emblem is reproduced in Henry Green, *Shakespeare and the Emblem Writers* (London: Trubner, 1870), p. 530.

38. George Wither, *A Collection of Emblemes, Ancient and Moderne (1635)*, ed. Rosemary Freeman (Columbia: University of South Carolina Press, 1975), p. 21

39. This was Donne's last sermon and referred to by the King's household as "The Doctor's own funeral sermon." It was titled "Death's Duell, or, A Consolation to the Soule against the dying Life and living Death of the Body," and was delivered at Whitehall, in the presence of the king, at the beginning of Lent, 1630.

40. See J. J. M. Tobin's introductory article to *Edward III* in G. Blakemore Evans et al., eds., *The Riverside Shakespeare*, 2nd Ed., pp. 1732-4.

41. The version used is that in G. Blakemore Evans et al., eds., *The Riverside Shakespeare*, 2nd Ed.

42. Harry Morris, in *Last Things in Shakespeare* (Tallahassee: Florida State University Press, 1985), suggests that Richard II may be regarded as one of "Shakespeare's sovereigns who are also high priests of their kingdom" (p. 256). He demonstrates how this idea is promulgated through Christ symbolism and through the explicit identification of the king as Christ's surrogate (pp. 256-7). My own argument has focused on the largely secular idealization of kingship (mainly broadcast through Gaunt's English encomium where Christian service and the spirit of chivalric reputation co-exist). It is interesting, and perhaps revealing of his lack of chivalric reputation, that Richard, facing rebellion and unable to marshal his military forces effectively, lays repeated emphasis on the religious validation of his office — and intriguing, too, that Bullingbrook views Richard's murder in terms of the primordial homicide, an act against the benignity of God rather than an act against the code of chivalric conduct.

43. Patricia L. Carlin, *Shakespeare's Mortal Men: Overcoming Death in History, Comedy and Tragedy* (New York: Peter Lang, 1993), p. 88.

44. Michael Neill, *Issues of Death: Mortality and Identity in English Renaissance Tragedy* (Oxford: Clarendon Press, 1997), p. 249.

Chapter 3

ഇൗരു

Iconic Monsters in Paradise

Henry IV's reign was notable more for its shadowy internal wranglings than for its golden foreign achievements. Even his burial was shrouded in intrigue, with rumors that his body had been mysteriously "lost" when the barge carrying it capsized on its way to Canterbury Cathedral. Some four hundred years later, the Age of Reason did what they thought to be the sensible thing and opened the tomb. And there lay King Henry, with crown, gown and scepter. Bullingbrook may have struck a rather dashing and alluringly romantic figure to Shakespeare's age but, as King Henry IV, he was decidedly less admired. At the heart of Elizabethan misgivings lay an obsessive fear of civil war. A succession of commentators bewailed its deformities, advocating the sanity of peace at home.[1]

Central to the notion of civil war's monstrosity in the Elizabethan psyche was the concept of regenerating evil, of evil that died only to revive again even more virulently. It was a regeneration typically conceptualized in terms of the classical monster, the Hydra of Lerna. Here, for example, is King Edgar in *A Knack to Know a Knave* (1594):

> Then as I am Gods Vicegerent [sic] here on earth,
> By Gods appointment heere to raigne and rule,

So must I seeke to cut abuses downe,
That lyke Hydras heads, daylie growes up one in anothers place,
Which if with good regard we looke not to,
We shall, lyke Sodom, feele that fierie doome,
That God in Justice did inflict on them.[2]

The destruction of the Hydra, the monstrous offspring of Typhon and Echidna, was the second task imposed upon Hercules by Eurystheus. No ordinary beast, Thomas Cooper describes it as "A mōster, with whom Hercules fought, and as soone as he had stricken of one head of the monster, an other sprang vp immediately."[3] It is understandable, then, that the Hydra's fatal breath and multiplying heads necessitated the outside help of Iolas, Hercules' trusty servant — the only task, in fact, that did require assistance. As Hercules lopped off a head, so Iolas seared the stump with a burning brand. Opinions differ as to the number of heads involved. Spenser talks of "his thousand heads,"[4] Cooper of "an hundred neckes with serpentine heads,"[5] Combe of a "seuen-headed beast."[6] The precise figure is not overly important. What is significant, though, is the notion of a specific evil reviving and multiplying from one wicked generation to the next. To the print of Hercules battling the Hydra, Thomas Combe appends these lines:

When Hercules had ordaind to take his rest,
And from his former labours him withdrew,
Hydra that monstrous seuen-headed beast
Against him came, his troubles to renew.[7]

As an image of regenerating evil, reiterated in a gamut of emblematic literature (and notably in the work of Bocchi, Sambucus and Tertio[8]), the sixteenth century had available to it few monstrous images more frightening and disturbing than the Hydra.

"Sexuality," as Kant observed in *Lectures on Ethics*, "exposes man to the danger of equality with the beasts."[9] Although the Hydra did not procreate in the normal conjunctive manner of most animal species, regenerative allusions to animals are generally deprecatory in early modern writings. Robert Watson has suggested that this was part of the culture of Shakespeare's age in which "human beings are encouraged to project their unacceptable mortality onto other animals."[10] This composed, as Watson suggests, part of the rhetoric of denial in which the baser instincts of human nature, like sexual reproduction itself, are consigned to a convenient scapegoat in the hope that "annihilation can be isolated in an Other" (p. 29). The idea links also to that postulated in the last chapter, namely that in Elizabethan and Jacobean writings the erotic impulse is traceable back to the physical predilections of the apes rather than to the divine inspiration of God. As a consequence, the linkage between human and animal sexualities is at least distasteful and usually repellent in Shakespeare's theatre. Calderwood cites the example of Iago's "beast with two backs" (*Othello* I.i.116-17), suggesting that "Only a professional degrader like Iago or a morbidly disillusioned prince like Hamlet will want to keep such images before him. For ordinary men animalistic sex and its mortal corollary must be vigorously repressed."[11] The reproductive characteristic of the Hydra, unwholesome because of the bestial undertones alone, assumes utmost moral repugnance through its association with the proliferating extremities of human wickedness.

Shakespeare's use of the Hydra is intriguing. In the classical myth there is no question about the moral resonances of the encounter between the hideous beast and Hercules. The Hydra represents unmitigated evil; the fact that in some versions of the story one of its heads was immortal served only to underscore the idea that evil may be subdued but never entirely conquered. Hercules, by contrast, stands for unambiguous virtue, the quintessence of mortal valor and wholesomeness in the face of regenerating evil. This is a key theme of a celebrated wall tapestry at Hampton Court Palace, west London, which reveals the various triumphs of Hercules, and situates his conquest of the Hydra as preeminent amongst them (*plate 9*). Yet, the first time Shakespeare deploys a coherent working of the Hydra myth (in the *Henry IV* plays), he deliberately undermines the moral polarities of the original story. This is the dissident Archbishop of York in *2 Henry IV*:

> But as I told my Lord of Westmerland,
> The time misord'red doth, in common sense,
> Crowd us and crush us to this monstrous form
> To hold our safety up. I sent your Grace
> The parcels and particulars of our grief,
> The which hath been with scorn shov'd from the court,
> Whereon this Hydra son of war is born. . . .
>
> (IV.ii.32-8)

There is a clear insinuation that Henry has himself given birth to the monster (line 38) and that he is, in some perverse manner, the heir to his own misdemeanors. The corruption of the notion of generational replenishment is also interesting. York, of course, is a rebel engaged in the process of civil war. His excuse is that "The time misord'red" has forced him and his colleagues into "this monstrous form."

The theme of self-protection through monstrosity is one prepared in *1 Henry IV* by Worcester who argues that Henry's oppression "Grew . . . to so great a bulk" that, for safety's sake, the rebels were forced to

> raise this present head,
> Whereby we stand opposed by such means
> As you yourself have forg'd against yourself
> (V.i.66-8)

Again, the insinuation of Worcester's pun on "head" is that Henry's own actions have given life to a distorted head-raising inheritance. The king has, Worcester claims, "forg'd" hydraic insurrection himself. Henry's moral claim to the throne, shadowed by the murder of Richard, lies at the heart of this debate. Both Worcester and York acknowledge that they are rebels, monstrous rebels even, but neither accepts that he is wrong. Hydraic rebellion, as they see it, is the fault of the royal party and not their own. If insurrection is hydraic, then it is a just, if horrible, monstrosity forced upon them by the dangers and scorn of the court. From the rebel perspective, at least, the "Hydra" does not accept the certainty of its wickedness or the moral propriety of its Herculean foeman.

These confusions become powerfully visualized in the final theatrical emblems of the play as Douglas, the would-be Hercules, encounters hydraically reviving kings. His function in this last act is carefully prepared through a meticulous construction of "super-mortality," initiated from the very first scene of the play. "That ever-valiant and approved Scot" (I.i.54); "that fiend Douglas" (II.iv.368); "renowned Douglas" (III.ii.107). He himself reprimands someone for talking about death: "Talk not of dying, I am out of fear / Of death or death's hand for this one half year" (IV.i.135-6). He is, by (almost) every account, the invincible warrior, the superlative mortal. When, at last, Douglas avows that he is the Herculean Hydra-subjugator, we could be forgiven for taking him at his word. Having killed Stafford and Blunt, who have been disguised as kings, he rounds on another king — this time the real one.

Another king? They grow like Hydra's heads.
I am the Douglas, fatal to all those
That wear those colors on them. What art thou
That counterfeit'st the person of a king?
(V.iv.25-8)

In invoking the persona of Hercules, Douglas makes not simply a soldierly claim but also a moral claim. The king has become the monster, the evil beast, and he the Herculean emissary of moral integrity charged with killing him.

Douglas' motivations here seem strange. Hitherto, the accent had been on bravery, valor, fiendish warriorship, military honor, renown. There was the sense that he had come for the fight, not for any inherently ethical reason. He is, after all, a Scot; a foreigner; a mercenary even. What has the question of English royal lineage to do with him? Yet, once he confronts the disguised kings, who seem to "grow like Hydra's heads," his words veritably bristle with homiletic righteousness. Rather like the hero of the Stoical version of Herculean myth, he puts brute strength and ignorance to the back-burner and pulls forward an exalted sense of virtue.[12] Of the slain Sir Walter Blunt he observes, with heavy irony: "A borrowed title has thou bought too dear" (V.iii.23); and of the king himself he demands "What art thou / That counterfeit'st the person of a king?" (V.iii.27-8). Patricia Carlin has offered an insightful discussion of the issues of counterfeiting in the play and has noted also that "Monetary imagery perfectly expresses the moral/material problem of finding an acceptable source of value."[13] Certainly the emphasis on pecuniary terminology ("borrowed," "bought," "dear," "counterfeit'st") places Douglas' words on an imagistic path that leads back not only to Falstaff's fiscal exploits on the highway near Gadshill but to the King's own "theft" of the crown — a righteous appropriation in Falstaff's symbolic portraiture, but, for the Douglas of Act V, an unmitigated larceny.

I have mentioned Falstaff here, and I would like to stay with him for a moment. His rôle in relation to the Hercules / Hydra myth is significant. He is the only person to qualify the tag of invincible warrior so readily attached to Douglas by others. As early as II.iv.342-4, it is he who lampoons the myth created around Douglas, talking of him as "that sprightly Scot of Scots, Douglas, that runs a' horseback up a hill perpendicular." The old rogue offers an interesting, and accurate, insight; but it becomes even more intriguing when we remember that Falstaff himself assumed Herculean pretensions earlier in the very same scene.[14] In II.iv of *1 Henry IV*, Falstaff presents his account of the Gadshill fiasco where his plan to mug rich travelers fails dismally. His narrative of the escapade is structured upon the Hercules / Hydra saga. How many has he slain? What begins as "two rogues in buckrom suits" (lines 192-3) grows to four (line 196), then to seven (line 201), then to nine (line 212) and ends as a veritable army of eleven men in buckram (line 218) all assailing the beleaguered hero. As if to lend weight to the hydraic nuance, Sir John pointedly brags in the same scene "Why, thou knowest I am as valiant as Hercules" (lines 270-1), and the monster motif is rekindled in the exchanges that follow. The Prince twice inveighs "O monstrous!" (lines 219 and 540), both in connection with Falstaff. Bardolph confesses at lines 312-13 (of Falstaff) "I blush'd to hear his monstrous devices"; and then, at lines 482-3, cries out that "the sheriff with a most monstrous watch is at the door" (significantly, this new monster also seeks confrontation with the "Herculean" Falstaff, but for reasons that cast a suitable irony on the paradigm's mythic pretensions!).

On stage, Falstaff's account of multiplying foes is essentially humorous, a parody of heroic action. No one, least of all Falstaff, believes this story of superlative heroism. In the Gadshill caricature, the innocent travelers, whom Falstaff would rob, are tongue-in-cheek styled as the Lernaean monsters and Falstaff, the robber, casts himself in the mold of Herculean hero. As obvious as the moral proprieties of this incident may be, and as transparent as the falsity of Falstaff's mythic pretensions may seem, the episode echoes yet again the more serious issues of the play. In the struggle for England's crown, the conundrum remains: on whose side falls the mantle of monstrosity, and on whose that of Herculean virtue?

With wry humor, Shakespeare brings together the two mythic pretenders, Douglas and Falstaff, in the last scene of the play and even pits them, head to head, in a farcical battle for glory on Shrewsbury field. It is a confrontation that, according to the stage directions, occurs almost simultaneously with the clash between Prince Hal and Hotspur. The outcome of both contests seems to be decisive. Hal defeats Hotspur; Douglas defeats Falstaff. To Hal goes the military victory; and, if the Herculean sonorities are authentic, to Douglas the moral victory. There are, of course, abundant reasons to suppose that the moral sonorities are not correct. For a start, Falstaff feigns death (a most un-Herculean strategy) and Douglas the superhuman is apparently fooled by the ploy.

In fact, Shakespeare goes to some lengths to demythologize the Herculean pretensions of the two men and the moral inferences of their presence in this last act. Within a few minutes Falstaff has hydraically revived, declaring vehemently that "I am no counterfeit" (V.iv.115), and immediately transforming himself into a Herculean Hydra-slayer once more. Having already claimed he had killed Percy (V.iii.46-7), Falstaff now stabs Hotspur's corpse and again reports that he has slain him (V.iv.140-3). This latest Herculean exploit, undertaken against Hotspur's miraculously reviving monstrosity, is calculated by Falstaff to secure him a material reward — most unlike the classical paradigm who, as a succession of Renaissance emblematists infer, asked for none. Douglas, too, escapes death but not demythologization. Within twenty lines of his Herculean boast, Shakespeare presents us with the stage picture of the would-be myth-hero running for his life and, in the next scene, we are given the ignominious details of his capture: "And falling from a hill, he was so bruis'd / That the pursuers took him" (V.v.21-2). While the physical contests of the play may be concluded definitively, issues of right and wrong are considerably more difficult to disentangle — as Shakespeare intended, no doubt.

The contest between Hal and Hotspur in the final act of *1 Henry IV*, and indeed between the king and his adversaries generally, has rightly been accorded extensive critical focus. Michael Neill argues that what he calls the "macabre art" is very much in evidence in Shakespeare's designs here.[15] Hal's reclamation of his honorable status, Neill maintains, is balanced by the specter of the dead Sir Walter Blunt (disguised as the king and killed by Douglas) whose demeanor in death, as Falstaff puts it, is one of "grinning honor" (V.iii.59) — a reference, no doubt, to the grinning skeleton of the *danse macabre* (p. 82). Neill suggests that "this transformation of the royal double into the sign of Death's authority anticipates an ending in which he Prince's own *alter ego*, Hotspur, having yielded to 'the earthy and cold hand of death', is transformed to 'dust / And food for . . . worms'" (p. 82). None, be he counterfeit or king or pauper or prince, may escape death. The thesis is an intriguing one, particularly in light of the sense of paradise and paradise lost for which I argued in the last chapter and will do again in this. It is though only half the story and where Neill's approach and my own differ is in the estimation of Hal's act of slaying Hotspur. Like Hotspur, Hal will die — the inevitable victim of Death's authority. But unlike Hotspur, Hal will find his immortality through chivalric reputation, through the very act of defeating Hotspur in a battle that reverberates with mythic resonances. Those resonances, it seems to me, are deliberately intensified and validated by the mock-heroics of both Douglas and Falstaff, the second of whom goes to considerable lengths to disavow at V.i.133-40 the kind of honor upon which the whole notion of an English heroic paradise is constructed:

> What is honor? A word. What is in that word honor? What is that honor? Air. A trim reckoning! Who hath it? He that died a' Wednesday. Doth he feel it? No. Doth he hear it? No. 'Tis insensible then? Yea, to the dead. But will['t] not live with the living? No. Why? Detraction will not suffer it. Therefore I'll none of it, honor is a mere scutcheon.

Alastair Fowler examines usefully the opposition of this idea not only to Hal's view of honor but to Shakespeare's broader understanding of the term, which is used more than a thousand times in his canon.[16] Our own age tends to view militarism with a suspicious eye, but we should be cautious in supposing that the philosophies of anyone as heterodox as Falstaff are necessarily intended for our approval.

From its outset, the first and final meeting between Hal and Hotspur on Shrewsbury field evidences a keen awareness of issues pertaining to lineage and inheritance:

> *Hotspur.* If I mistake not, thou art Harry Monmouth.
> *Prince.* Thou speak'st as if I would deny my name.
> *Hotspur.* My name is Harry Percy.
> *Prince.*   Why then I see
> A very valiant rebel of the name.
> I am Prince of Wales, and think not, Percy,
> To share with me in glory any more.
> Two stars keep not their motion in one sphere,
> Nor can one England brook a double reign
> Of Harry Percy and the Prince of Wales.
> (*1 Henry IV* V.iv.59-67)

This is reminiscent of the emphasis on Talbot's "name" in *1 Henry VI*. A name is a statement of identity, and lineage is an important part of identity. Both men assert their names but Harry identifies himself tellingly. He is the "Prince of Wales," a title that can be held only by the first in line to the throne. As such, Hal claims moral propriety as heir to the throne, as inheritor of his father's crown. Since Hotspur challenges his legitimacy, there can be only a single consequence for it has become an impossibility for both men to live in the same world. If Hal will be king, then Hotspur must die. Hal's "title" as monarchical inheritor has been implicitly challenged earlier in the play when Hotspur refers to him as "Harry Monmouth" (V.ii.49). Bache and Loggins have pointed out that this "designates his rôle as the king's son" but not necessarily as the heir to the throne.[17] Here, again, in their physical encounter, Hotspur refers to Harry as "Harry Monmouth" (V.iv.59), reiterating the idea that questions of inheritance are foremost in both men's minds.

We have seen already that Shakespeare's notion of heroic renewal is not only physical but spiritual as well. Not spiritual in the Biblical meaning of the word but spiritual in the sense of chivalric excellence. When Hotspur lies beaten and dying on the earth of Shrewsbury field, and Hal stands triumphant before him, his words point precisely to this issue:

> O Harry, thou has robbed me of my youth!
> I better brook the loss of brittle life
> Than those proud titles thou hast won of me.
> They wound my thoughts worse than thy sword my flesh.
> (*1 Henry IV* V.iv.77-80)

His youth *is* his reputation. It is the time when a man, in the great cycle of heroic English regeneration, wins his place in the chronicle. This sense of a place lost in the familial chivalric pageant is succinctly expressed by Charlemont in Tourneur's *The Atheist's Tragedy*, after his father has tried to dissuade him from entering the wars:

> Your predecessors were your precedents,
> And you are my example. Shall I serve
> For nothing but a vain parenthesis
> I' the honoured story of your family?
> Or hang but like an empty scutcheon
> Between the trophies of my predecessors,
> And the rich arms of my posterity?
> (I.ii.17-23)[18]

Behind Charlemont's plea lies the presumption that he *can* earn a noble
place between the rich trophies of his predecessors and the rich arms of
his posterity. This intention, as Charlemont himself discovers, is liable
to frustration and unheroic diminution.

Hotspur makes a similar discovery. He has entered his war and lost;
he becomes merely a parenthesis to a greater march of history. In
Shakespeare's scheme of heroic renewal we have already seen many
instances of youth reviving, or being invited to revive, the glories of
ancestry. This is perhaps where Hotspur perceives his own failure. In
falling to the sword of Harry, the myth of his soldierly preeminence,
expressed time and again in the play, has been shattered. And, as important
as that, with his death has come to an end the cyclical process of familial
honor. Perhaps he is being a bit hard on himself. But, then, chivalry
had its own etiquette, and Hotspur's reading of the situation is apparently
affirmed by Harry. Drifting into oblivion, Hotspur's final sentence is
completed by his foeman.

> *Hotspur.*   life, time's fool,
> And time, that takes survey of all the world,
> Must have a stop. O, I could prophesy,
> But that the earthy and cold hand of death
> Lies on my tongue. No, Percy, thou art dust,
> And food for —   [*Dies.*]
> *Prince.*   For worms, brave Percy.
>   (*1 Henry IV* V.iv.81-6)

Harry Morris understands Hotspur's words as an acceptance that "a man
can dazzle the world only in the time of his life"[19] but life, of course,
must end. Seeking only an earthly reward rather than a religious one,
Morris concludes, Hotspur inherits only "two paces of the vilest earth"
(V.iv.91). More likely, it seems to me, Hotspur here implicitly
acknowledges that he has lost eternity precisely because he has *not* dazzled
in his time on earth, and that his reputation, in the manner of the English
heroic myth, will not live beyond physical mortality. That failure is
finally and conclusively summated by his defeat at the hands of Hal. In
this regard it is revealing that Hotspur chooses, on one of the few occasions
in the play, to address himself as Percy: "No, Percy, thou art dust."
Percy, not Hotspur. His allusion is to the familial name; he refers to
himself but also, through the name, to his ancestral lineage. It is the

family name that has become dust because heroic regeneration has been foiled.

There is, though, a regenerative process of sorts here. The worms. Percy's body will certainly provide the food for their regeneration. In this repulsive presentation of the life-in-death theme, just as in the benign version, Shakespeare echoes popular religious iconography — though not, on this occasion, from the emblem books. In the Wakeman Cenotaph in Tewkesbury Abbey, Gloucestershire, the sixteenth century alabaster effigy of Abbot Wakeman presents a decaying cadaver with stone worms crawling through the "rotting" joints (*plate 10*).[20] The tomb is covered in graffiti, much of it from the sixteenth century, so it was clearly a popular tourist destination in Shakespeare's day. The Abbey also had strong associations with royalty and the Wars of the Roses, leading one commentator to describe it as

> an acre sown indeed
> with the richest, royallest seed.[21]

A lesser known parallel to the Wakeman Cenotaph is a mid-sixteenth century brass floor plaque at St. Andrew's Church, Oddington, a popular stop-over on the road from London to Stratford. Commemorating the life of Ralph Hamsterley, it depicts him as a shrouded cadaver out of whose eye-sockets, joints and stomach cavity crawl a seething mass of worms (*plate 11*). A scroll issuing from the skeletal mouth reads (translated from the Latin): "To worms am I given up and, thus, give the warning / That just as I am here toppled, so is all earthly honor overthrown." These bizarre representations were clearly aimed at devaluing the notion of transient mortality and extolling the virtues of spiritual eternity. They endorsed the frequent allusions to "Wormes Meate" and such like in non-emblematic literatures, and it is entirely feasible that Shakespeare exploited the iconic dimensions of such images to encourage an array of unwholesome associations in the minds of his Elizabethan audience. They carried with them, as well, an acute sense of "life-cycle," of the destruction of one physical entity by and to the advantage of another. For the worms to flourish, life must end; for Hal to survive, Hotspur must perish. The life-in-death bell tolls with dissonant irony.

* * * * *

An integral part of Gaunt's vision of a heroically regenerating English paradise was the notion of England as the "seat of Mars" (II.i.41). Elizabethan literati had good cause to celebrate the place of the war god in their mythopoeic encomium. They had it on the authority of Geoffrey of Monmouth's *Historia Britonum* that, looking upon the shores of Britain, Julius Caesar himself had declared that the Romans and the British had a common Trojan origin, and that Brutus had founded Britain, just as Aeneas had founded Rome, after both had fled the destruction of Troy.[22] Since Mars was the patron of Rome and the esteemed father of Romulus, the ancient founder of that great city, it was perfectly natural for the Elizabethans to take a strong interest in his mythography — more so since the god was the sometime defender of Troy and the notion of London as the "New Troy" (*Troynovant*) had been espoused at least since the thirteenth century and reiterated frequently, most authoritatively perhaps in Caxton's *Chronycles of Englande*.[23] As the logical sequitur to a historical mythography of inheritance, pre-Elizabethan cosmography sought further to decipher the English temperament in Martian terms. Richard Argol, for example, describes the planet Mars as the controller of war-like England, and as the determinant of the English military disposition.[24]

The English Mars was not the barbaric and destructive Mars Ultor described in Stephen Batman's *The Golden Booke of the Leaden Goddes* (1577), the sixteenth century English vulgate of classical lore, who when he "inuadeth, all thinges are lefte desolate, & destroyed."[25] Nor is he necessarily that Mars who Bel-Imperia in *The Spanish Tragedy* automatically associates with war: "where Mars reigneth, there must needs be war" (II.iv.35).[26] Sixteenth century England had engineered a particular kind of Mars as its patron, a sort of anglicized Mars. This native English Mars had a split personality. At home, he was the preserver of peace, the protector of the English realm; abroad he was the irresistible warrior. This function is well illustrated at Hampton Court Palace where a statue of Mars guards the central entrance of the Fountain Court (south facade). In this ancient seat of English monarchy, originally gifted to Henry VIII by Cardinal Wolsey, Mars symbolizes the defense of the realm against outward attack, a function reiterated by the menacing death's head depicted at the base of his shield. In sum, he was the consummate and advised warrior, whether he be defending at home or conquering abroad. The anglicized Mars, god of English war, is central to the revivification of paradise. He is that thread of immortality that finds earthly perpetuity through the cyclically repeating glories of individual English beings. Such beings, though themselves physically mortal and therefore transient, have yet the power to carry the mantel of superlative warriorship for their short space on earth, and to pass it on to their physical inheritors, their sons and their daughters, whose task it is in turn to replenish the myth and deliver it to their offspring.

The English Mars is proverbially guided by the wise counsel of the Roman goddess Minerva (the Greek goddess Pallas). Gerard Leigh in 1583 writes of the anglicized war-god as Pallas' knight, "an armed Mars, A champion pollitique in fielde to fight, or at home to defende."[27] William Wyrley, in *The Trve Vse of Armorie* quotes a great English soldier as declaring: "For highly was my knightly seruice deemd, / As well for Mars as prudent Pallas grace."[28] The position is summarized admirably by Henry Peacham in *Minerva Britanna*:

> Though Mars defendes the kingdome with his might,
> And braues abroad his foe, in glorious armes,
> Yet wiser Pallas guides his arme aright,
> And best at home preuentes all future harmes.[29]

This idea of Mars tutored by the wisdom of Pallas at home and abroad was not an English invention, though it was zealously adapted to local conditions. Its roots are classical; and its representation in art was familiar across Renaissance Europe. Rubens' painting "Mars pushed back by Hercules and Minerva" is perhaps the most celebrated example of such, with Hercules and Minerva restraining Mars as he attempts to drag a woman (representing Peace) by the hair.[30] Similarly, a sixteenth century etching in the New York Metropolitan Museum, after Tintoretto and titled "Minerva expelling Mars," shows Minerva urging Mars to assuage his violent intentions, positioning herself protectively between the war god and two female figures, symbolizing Peace and Abundance.[31] For the Elizabethans there was an obvious familial example for the dual Mars figure. York recalls in *Richard II*:

> the Black Prince, that young Mars of men. . . .
> (II.iii.101)

The Black Prince was the consummate home defender, and a foreign conqueror *par excellence*. The context of the utterance is important.

York is upbraiding Bullingbrook for bringing civil war onto English
soil. He remembers how he and Bullingbrook's father had rescued the
Black Prince from "forth the ranks of many thousand French." It is
foreign conquest that wins the colors of an English Mars, not the fomenting
of civil strife.

If the genuine "Pallas souldier," to expand Gerard Leigh's comment,
is "an armed Mars, A champion pollitique in fielde to fight, or at home
to defende, An ordered Iusticer without respect," then how does the
newly ascended Henry V, the physical inheritor of Edward III and the
Black Prince, measure up to the English myth? At the end of *2 Henry
IV*, Falstaff had been banished from the new king's company and the
Chief Justice firmly embraced. That must be a good sign. And the
Archbishop of Canterbury, at the outset of *Henry V*, ardently asserts the
nature of the transformation:

> Consideration like an angel came
> And whipt th' offending Adam out of him,
> Leaving his body as a paradise
> T' envelop and contain celestial spirits.
>
> (I.i.28-31)

Remember, this is the Archbishop speaking, the highest religious officer
in the land, so he ought to know a thing or two about Adam and paradise.
And he has no doubt that Hal's contemplative experiences have
transformed him radically. His body has become the imagistic symbol
of England as a second Eden, an embracing paradise. The sense of the
king *as* England has been mooted once before. This is how Margaret
consoles Richard in *Richard II*: "Ah, thou, the model where old Troy
did stand" (V.i.11). She images him as the ruins of Troy, the remnants
of what England was before insurrection destroyed his paradise. It's all
a matter of opinion, sure enough, but Richard's party needs little
convincing that Bullingbrook is the barbarous Greek who has shattered
England's New Troy.

Momentarily, this takes us down a disturbing associative line. If it is
Bullingbrook who is the decimator of paradise, then surely the principle
of malign regeneration that is so powerful in Shakespeare's earlier History
plays might suggest his son, his inheritor, may also emerge as a decimator
of paradise. Not so, Canterbury assures us; the young man has reformed
and is now the very essence of paradise itself. Certainly, the omens are

good. Not only is Henry aiming at an ambitious foreign campaign but he is taking steps to preserve the kingdom's peace. Interestingly, in Holinshed's original chronicle of this episode, it is not Henry but Rafe Neville, the Earl of Westmoreland, who raises the matter of protection from the Scots.[32] Shakespeare's "complete king," on the other hand, comes to that sage conclusion without the help of counsel. This, as Henry's advocates may point out, is a refreshing change. The problem with Richard's regime, allegedly, was that the "England, that was wont to conquer others, / Hath made a shameful conquest of itself" (*Richard II* II.i.65-6). It comes as little surprise that within the first few lines of *Henry V* the link with Mars is both re-established and re-affirmed.

> O for a Muse of fire, that would ascend
> The brightest heaven of invention!
> A kingdom for a stage, princes to act,
> And monarchs to behold the swelling scene!
> Then should the warlike Harry, like himself,
> Assume the Port of Mars, and at his heels
> Leash'd in like hounds, should famine, sword, and fire
> Crouch for employment.
>
> (Prologue 1-8)

In the writings of Samuel Daniel, frequently a source for Shakespeare, the (pagan) Mars is described as the "Muse-foe Mars."[33] In the Prologue, Shakespeare moves tellingly in the opposite direction. He longs for a poetic "Muse of fire" so that he could more persuasively describe the thrilling scene of Harry assuming "the Port of Mars." Even so, there are frightening dimensions to this Mars-like Harry. After all, he is about to engage in foreign conquest and, as a foreign conqueror, it is only appropriate that famine, sword and fire should "Crouch for employment" at his heels. These are the constructs of war — but note that they are "Leash'd in like hounds." This anglicized Martian, unlike his Classical namesake, is distinguished by discipline.

By the end of the first act, an impressive profile has been established of the ideal English monarch embarking on a campaign to revive the glories of his ancestors and of England. The moral aspects of invading France are affirmed, regardless of whether or not we accept the Salic argument; appropriate parallels have been drawn to the exploits of Edward III and the Black Prince; and Harry has been ensconced as an anglicized

Mars archetype. He is the regenerative successor, the heroic life-in-death, of his ancestors. There is a slight hiccup on the home front when Grey, Scroop and Cambridge are caught in conspiracy against the crown. In a rather extravagant declamation, the king labels them in suitably monstrous terms: "English monsters!" (II.ii.85), "inhuman creature[s]" (II.ii.95); and he goes on to lament that "this revolt of thine, methinks, is like / Another fall of man" (II.ii.141-2). The defilers of paradise are duly dispatched to the execution block, and the interruption soon forgotten.

The journey to what should be the fulfillment of the Mars myth, and the ultimate fulfillment of the idea of heroic life inheriting the spirit and replicating the feats of heroic ancestral dead, takes the English army through Harfleur, Picardy and finally to the battle field at Agincourt — all of these emotive names to an Elizabethan audience enculturated in notions of English greatness on French soil. The astonishing victory at Agincourt is preceded by a series of Mars allusions:

> *Dieu de batailles!* where have they this mettle?
> Is not their climate foggy, raw, and dull,
> On whom, as in despite, the sun looks pale,
> Killing their fruit with frowns? Can sodden water,
> A drench for sur-rein'd jades, their barley-broth,
> Decoct their cold blood to such valiant heat?
>> (The French Constable speaking
>> of the English, III.v.15-20)

> O God of battles, steel my soldiers' hearts,
> Possess them not with fear! Take from them now
> The sense of reckoning, if th' opposed numbers
> Pluck their hearts from them.
>> (Harry, IV.i.289-92)

> Big Mars seems bankrout in their beggar'd host,
> And faintly through a rusty beaver peeps:
>> (Grandpré speaking of the English, IV.ii.43-4)

Few things would have pleased the Elizabethans more than praise from the French. Raleigh, for example, was fond of quoting John de Serre's celebration of English soldiership; others, including Shakespeare, looked to Froissart. There was something particularly satisfying in the notion of a cocky Frenchman having to admit that, yes, the English were better soldiers after all. So, the Constable's awed account of English valor in the battle for Harfleur would have gone down well with a London audience. Equally, Grandpré's arrant miscalculation of English heroism, suggesting that Mars was "bankrout in their beggar'd host," would have raised English hackles to new elevations and urged on that moment when the Gallic cur would have to eat his words. In the event, death at Agincourt spares him that ignominy.

Harry's appeal to Mars is intriguing. The parallel passage in Edward Hall's chronicle reads as follows: "Therefore puttynge your onely truste in hym, let not their multytude feare youre heartes, nor their great noumbre abate your courages."[34] Hall has the king addressing the Lord God at this point, not the God of War. Holinshed equally has Harry appealing to God, not Mars.[35] The king's petition in *Henry V* is one offered in a strangely detached manner — as if somehow we have moved away from the anglicized certainty of England as the "seat of Mars" and into a more tentative landscape where the patronage of Mars cannot be relied upon and where glory is not necessarily English. This is a curious movement because it contrasts so forcefully with the assertions of the Prologue at the beginning of the play. There, Harry *was* Mars. Famine, sword and fire crouched at his feet for employment. He was all-powerful, all-seeing. Now, he is something less than that. The diminution in his stature is discernible also in his address to the inhabitants of Harfleur at III.iii. He warns the townspeople to surrender while they still can:

> Therefore, you men of [Harfleur],
> Take pity of your town and of your people,
> Whiles yet my soldiers are in my command,
> Whiles yet the cool and temperate wind of grace
> O'erblows the filthy and contagious clouds
> Of deadly murther, spoil and villany.
> If not — why, in a moment look to see
> The blind and bloody soldier with foul hand
> Defile the locks of your shrill-shrieking daughters;
> Your fathers taken by the silver beards,
> And their most reverend heads dash'd to the walls;
> Your naked infants spitted upon pikes,
> Whiles the mad mothers with their howls confus'd
> Do break the clouds, as did the wives of Jewry
> At Herod's bloody-hunting slaughter-men.
>   (III.iii.27-41)

Compare this to Tamburlaine's address to the Damascan Virgins, following the fall of their city. As the aldermen of Harfleur were to do, the Damascan city fathers had refused the opportunity to surrender:

> Your fearful minds are thick and misty,
> For there sits death; there sits imperious Death
> Keeping his circuit by the slicing edge.
> But I am pleas'd you shall not see him there;
> He now is seated on my horsemen's spears,
> And on their points his fleshless body feeds.
> Techelles, straight go charge a few of them
> To charge these dames, and shew my servant Death,
> Sitting in scarlet on their armed spears.
>
> (*Tamburlaine, Part 1* IV.ii.47-55)[36]

His last words here order the execution of the virgins, an act rapidly effected despite their terrified supplications for mercy. Barbarous, perhaps, Tamburlaine's inflexible "discipline of arms and chivalry" (V.ii.112) also carries with it the sense of the magical. His "servant Death" flits from slicing edge to spear point — commanded only by the whim of Tamburlaine's imaginative sleight of hand — until, at the last, his pun on "charge" effortlessly transposes fantasy into fatality.

That sense of command and control that Tamburlaine espouses so tellingly here is almost entirely absent in Hal's conceptualization of death to the townsfolk of Harfleur. There, his promise of universal destruction is one predicated on the claim that there will come a point when he has no control over his men. They will become as Death soldiers, mowing all before them — and he without power to stop them. The specter he presents of raped daughters, impaled infants, and wailing mothers is a grim caricature of the control that the opening prologue had promised us. Here is a picture of the English soldier, "the blind and bloody soldier with foul hand," wantonly defiling an innocent landscape and barbarizing its women and children. Tamburlaine, by contrast, is the master of Death. Disturbing, too, is the comparison to Herod's "bloody-hunting slaughter-men." It seems as though we are moving away from a spiritualized landscape of ordered foreign conquest into a pagan domain. In an analysis of the hermeneutics of conquest in *Henry V*, William M. Hawley has argued that Hal is both hero and tyrant and that the threats of rape before Harfleur are part of his tyranny.[37] The image is certainly disquieting but I am less convinced that Hal has sufficient control of this situation to be labeled tyrannous. It seems to me that Shakespeare is articulating, and Henry is "experiencing," the disintegration of an English mythology of presumed heroism. The actuality of war is assuming an unpalatability of which Henry is aware but in the face of which he retains only marginal influence. Far from becoming the heroic anglicized Mars warrior paradigm abroad, reactivating and giving new life to the heroic splendors of a famous ancestry, Harry's English army is coming to represent an uncontrollable monstrosity, repeating its infamies in the march across France.

After Grandpré's misjudged reference to the absence of Mars amongst the English host, the war god is not mentioned again. In a stark inversion of the momentum that had been gathering at least since *Richard II*, the idea of the conquering English soldier abroad becomes synonymous not with the achievement of paradise but with its destruction. The Duke of Burgundy, pleading for Peace and Abundance, reminds us of Minerva beseeching Mars Ultor to spare the trembling damsels of Peace and Abundance in Rubens' painting or the Tintorettan etching:

>   let it not disgrace me,
> If I demand, before this royal view,
> What rub or what impediment there is,
> Why that the naked, poor, and mangled Peace,
> Dear nurse of arts, plenties, and joyful births,
> Should not in *the best garden of the world*,
> Our fertile France, put up her lovely visage?
> Alas, she hath from France too long been chas'd,
> And all her husbandry doth lie on heaps,
> Corrupting in its own fertility.
>
>   (V.ii.31-40, emphasis added.)

The best garden of the world? France? At the end of the same scene the Chorus, that most patriotic of observers, concludes the work with a similar claim, referring to France as "the world's best garden" (V, Epilogue, 7). We have come a long way from the idea of England as a demi-paradise, basking in its native peace and reveling in forays abroad. Instead, fertile France has become the new Eden, the "nurse of arts, plenties, and joyful births." And within its bounds, the benign processes of regeneration have been subverted and perverted by the English invaders to the point where now "all her husbandry doth lie on heaps, / Corrupting in its own fertility." It is now the English who have become the harbingers of corruption, the marauding Mars figures who lack the tutelage of Minerva and, as a consequence, have devolved into indiscriminate savagery. In the same speech, Burgundy goes on to offer a gamut of unwholesome references to the destruction of the beauteous garden: "disorder'd" (l. 44), "savagery" (l. 47), "uncorrected" (l. 50), "rank" (l. 50), "hateful" (l. 52). The English harmony of Mars and Minerva has been abandoned in this vandalizing of the French paradise, and Burgundy's words underscore the Classical tradition of Mars as the arch-enemy of Peace and Abundance, pointedly disavowing the English notion of Mars as the protector of paradise and styling him instead as its indiscriminate destroyer. Far from articulating the consummation of a glorious life-in-death panoply of reviving English greatness, the ultimate momentum of the play is characterized by stagnancy and death, a fact hauntingly reiterated by reference in its last lines to the marriage of Henry and Kate and the tragic reign of Henry VI, their son and heir.

* * * * *

The life-in-death theme in the English Histories was essentially an effort to create a valued and human permanence amidst the desolation of a fallen world. The central thesis behind this endeavor relied on the simple corollary of peace at home and heroic conquest abroad. The ideal English hero, be he king or foot soldier, was understood as a Mars-type warrior, sauntering forth from the haven of an English paradise and, having conquered foreigners, returning home to enjoy and preserve the peace and plenty of a second Eden. The historic paradigms — Edward III, the Black Prince, Richard I, but also the ordinary superlative soldier of English myth — all appeared, through the flattering prism of Tudor history, to have established and validated exactly this cycle.

Paola Pugliatti asks the seminal question: "if Henry V is intended to be perceived as the perfect Christian prince, why do so many voices, more or less directly and overtly, condemn his military venture and denounce the violence of the war so convincingly?"[38] The voice of this chapter has sounded in a similar direction, affirming Shakespeare's change of intention through his manipulation of the life-in-death theme in relation to the theme of heroic English regeneration. The debilitation of the myth is hinted at in the First Tetralogy, even as attempts are being made to articulate it, and further nuanced in the motifs of repeating monstrosity in *Henry IV*. But the full scope of its failure is preserved for *Henry V*, where the opportunity to exercise the "peace at home, conquest abroad" theorem founders, it seems, on the actuality of war and its cruel ways. In the end, the human detail of foreign conquest turns out to be every bit as unsavory and diminishing as that of civil war. The idea that death can be defied by a reviving and repeating cycle of mortal greatness stumbles in Shakespeare's increasingly unwholesome dissection of the very nature of greatness itself. In truth, Shakespeare's theatre does no more than articulate explicitly the realities of war. Despite the brutalities of his French campaign, the Black Prince was still heralded as the very essence of chivalry, his failings filtered out by the sanitizing lens of Tudor history. When Shakespeare comes to define the supposed glories of Edward's illustrious inheritor, Henry V, he moves towards a more pessimistic and cautious understanding of an epoch that the popular but ill-informed imagination had long idealized.

Notes

1. For example, Samuel Daniel, in "The Epistle Dedicatorie" to *The Civile Wares betweene the Howses of Lancaster and Yorke* (London: 1595, first publ.; Simon Waterson, 1609), his verse account of the civil war, purposes "to shewe the deformities of ciuile Dissension" (sig. A2v); and Thomas Lodge, in *The Wounds of Civil War*, ed. Joseph W. Houppert (London: Edward Arnold, 1969), draws, as the Elizabethans were apt to do, on the precedent of Italy. The setting and characters may be Roman, but the lesson on "unnaturalness" is distinctly English: "Brute beasts nill break the mutual law of love, / And birds affection will not violate; / The senseless trees have concord 'mongst themselves, / And stones agree in links of amity" (I.i.260-3).

2. *A Knack to Know a Knave* (1594; facsimile rpt. Oxford: The University Press, The Malone Society Reprints, 1963), sig. A2r.

3. Thomas Cooper, *Thesavrvs Lingvae Romanae & Britannicae tam accurate congestus, vt nihil pene in eo desyderari possit, quod vel Latine complectatur amplissimus Stephani Thesaurus, vel Anglice, toties aucta Eliotae Bibliotheca* (London: 1565), sig. 7G3r.

4. Edmund Spenser, *The Faerie Queene*, ed. Thomas P. Roche (Harmondsworth: Penguin Books, 1978), VI.xii.32.

5. Cooper, sig. 7G1r.

6. Guillaume de la Perrière, *The Theater of fine devices, containing an hundred morall emblemes*, trans. Thomas Combe (1593, first publ.; London: R. Field, 1614), emblem XCIX. The original French edition appeared on the continent in 1540.

7. Combe, emblem XCIX.

8. Achille Bocchi, *Symbolicarum Quaestionum, De vniuerso genere, quas serio ludebat, Libri Qvinqve* (1555, first publ.; Bononiae, apud Societatem Typographiae Bononiensis, 1574), bk. 2, p. 22 foll. and bk. 3, p. 92 foll. Joannes Sambucus, *Emblemata, cum aliquot nummis antiqui operis, Ioannis Sambuci Tirnaviensis Pannonii* (Antwerpiae: ex officina Christophori Plantini, 1564), p. 138. Francesco Tertio, *Austriacae Gentis Imagines* (1558, first publ.; Venetiis et Oeniponti: Formis Gaspari ab Avibus, 1573), plate titled "Philippus Cathol Resc Hisp."

9. Quoted in James L. Calderwood, *Shakespeare and the Denial of Death* (Amherst: University of Massachusetts Press, 1987), p. 49.

10. Robert Watson, *The Rest Is Silence: Death as Annihilation in the English Renaissance* (Berkeley: University of California Press, 1994), p. 30.

11. Calderwood, p. 50.

12. Following the later Stoics and Cynics, emblematists like Andrea Alciatus, for example, avoided focusing on the physical achievements of Hercules (i.e. the brute strength and ignorance that characterized some of the Twelve

Labors), and instead stylized Hercules' remarkable feats as illustrations of *cerebral* triumphs of morality or ingenuity.

13. Patricia L. Carlin, *Shakespeare's Mortal Men: Overcoming Death in History, Comedy and Tragedy* (New York: Peter Lang, 1993), p. 67.

14. See Clayton G. MacKenzie, "Falstaff's Monster," *AUMLA: Journal of the Australasian Universities MLA*, 83 (1995), pp. 83-6.

15. Michael Neill, *Issues of Death: Mortality and Identity in English Renaissance Tragedy* (Oxford: Clarendon Press, 1997), pp. 81-3.

16. Alastair Fowler, *Time's Purpled Masquers: Stars and the Afterlife in Renaissance English Literature* (Oxford: Clarendon Press, 1996), p. 115.

17. William B. Bache and Vernon P. Loggins, *Shakespeare's Deliberate Art* (Lanham, New York, & London: The University Press of America, 1996), p. 96.

18. Cyril Tourneur, *The Atheist's Tragedy* in *John Webster and Cyril Tourneur: Four Plays*, ed. John Addington Symonds (New York: Hill and Wang, 1966).

19. Harry Morris, in *Last Things in Shakespeare* (Tallahassee: Florida State University Press, 1985), p. 261.

20. For a discussion of the so-called "monumental body" see Nigel Llewellyn, *The Art of Death: Visual Culture in the English Death Ritual c. 1500 - c. 1800* (London: Reaktion Books, in association with the Victoria and Albert Museum, 1991), pp. 101-8.

21. The lines are quoted, without attribution, in Lionel Gough's *A Short Guide to the Abbey Church of St. Mary the Virgin at Tewkesbury*, 5th Ed. (Tewkesbury: Friends of Tewkesbury Abbey, 1991), p. 9. The Abbey was famous for the confrontation between Abbot Strensham and the Yorkist king, Edward IV, who had his brothers George of Clarence and Richard of Gloucester (later Richard III) by his side. Lancastrian pikemen, fleeing after the Battle of Tewkesbury, took refuge in the Abbey and the Yorkists entered the sacred precincts intending to kill them. The Abbot, who was saying high mass at the time, walked the length of the Abbey, holding the Bible aloft, and demanded that the carnage cease. The Royal party complied, agreeing that if the Lancastrians surrendered they would be unharmed. Such was the brutality of the Wars of the Roses that, having surrendered, most of the Lancastrians were marched 400 yards up the road to Tewkesbury Cross and executed. Ironically, George of Clarence, later murdered by his own brother, came to be buried in Tewkesbury Abbey, in a vault behind the altar and just a few yards from where the Wakeman Cenotaph now stands. And so, too, young Edward, the Prince of Wales, who had hoped to emulate the feats of his famous grandfather, Henry V, and "win our ancient right in France again, / Or die a soldier as I liv'd a king" (*Richard III* III.i.92-3), lies buried beneath a simple brass plaque in the middle of the choir.

22. Geoffrey of Monmouth, *Historia Britonum*, ed. J. A. Giles (London: D. Nutt, 1844), p. 2: "Hercle ex eadem prosapia nos Romani et Britones orti sumus, quia ex Trojana gente processimus. Nobis Aeneas post destructionem Trojae primus pater fuit: illis vero Brutus, quem Silvius Ascanii filii Aeneae filius progenuit." Translation: "In truth we Romans and the Britons have the same origin, since both are descended from the Trojan race. Our first father, after the destruction of Troy, was Aeneas; theirs Brutus, whose father was Sylvius, the son of Ascanius, the son of Aeneas." G. H. Gerould, in his article "King Arthur and Politics," *Speculum*, 2 (1927), p. 34, believes that Geoffrey issued his history between 1136 and 1138.

23. Caxton, Biiii, p. 4.

24. Argol is here writing in a prefatory address to the reader in Gerard Leigh's (sometimes Legh) *The Accedence of Armorie* (London: 1562, first publ.; R. Tottel, 1591), sig. A5v: "For this our clime being subiect to Mars ... the people naturally must yeeld such effects, as that mighty planet imprinteth in these inferiour bodies his subiects. For as the heauens haue ruled old the earth, an vnmoueable masse, with their beneficiall effects: so in this our region, the fire of honour mounting by martiall prowes, the chiefe aduancer of gentry, must of force so long last in this nation, as matter minstred from aboue maintaineth it."

25. Stephen Batman, *The Golden Booke of the Leaden Goddes* (1577 rpt. New York & London: Garland Publishing, Inc., 1976), sig. 6r.

26. Thomas Kyd's *The Spanish Tragedy*, ed. J. R. Mulryne, in *Elizabethan and Jacobean Tragedies: A New Mermaid Anthology*, introduced by Brian Gibbons (Tonbridge, Kent: Ernest Benn, 1984).

27. Leigh, fol. 129v.

28. Wyrley, p. 135.

29. Henry Peacham, *Minerva Britanna: Or A Garden of Heroycal Devices* (London: Wa. Dight, 1612), p. 44.

30. Rubens' painting "Mars pushed back by Hercules and Minerva" is housed in the Real Academie de San Fernando, Madrid, Spain.

31. The etching is reproduced as plate 57 in Eric Newton's *Tintoretto* (Longmans, Green and Co., 1952). Evelyn March Phillipps, in *Tintoretto* (London: Methuen, 1911), p. 103, compares this print to Tintoretto's "The Three Graces," and concludes that "The figure 'Minerva expelling Mars' while Venice feasts with Peace and Concord, among vines and fruits, has the same happy idyllic note." See, also: Goltzius' engraving, after Hendrik Goltzius, catalogued by Adam Bartsch, *Le Peintre Graveur* (Leipzig: J.A. Barth, 1866), p. 122, no. 1: "Pallas assise sous un pavillon au milieu de plusieurs guerriers"; and Vincenzo Cartari's *Le Imagini de i Dei de gli Antichi* (Venice: 1571), popularized in England through Richard Linche's 1599 translation (published in London), which presents an armed Minerva emerging from Jupiter's brain (opposite p. 458).

32. *Holinshed's Chronicle*, ed. Allardyce & Josephine Nicoll (London: Dent, 1965), p. 73 (iii.546): "Rafe Neuill, earle of Westmerland, and as then lord Warden *of* the *marches against Scot*land, vnderstanding that the king, vpon a couragious desire to recouer his right in France, would suerlie take the wars in hand, thought good to mooue the king to begin first with Scotland."
33. Samuel Daniel, *Delia* (London: J. Charlwood for Simon Waterson, 1592), sig. G2v.
34. The comparison is made by John H. Walter, ed., *King Henry V* (London: Methuen, 1970), note to IV.i.295-8.
35. *Holinshed's Chronicle*, p. 78 (iii.552-3).
36. Christopher Marlowe, *The Complete Plays*, ed. J. B. Steane.
37. William M. Hawley, *Critical Hermeneutics and Shakespeare's History Plays* (New York: Peter Lang, 1992), p. 121.
38. Paola Pugliatti, *Shakespeare the Historian* (New York: St. Martin's Press, 1996), p. 49.

Chapter 4

℘◯℘

De Morte et Amore

B etween them, Cupid and Death composed an intriguing duo in
sixteenth century iconography.[1] In Wolfgang Hunger's 1542 edition
of *Emblemata* there is a print entitled "Das absterben einer schoenen
frawen" (the death of a beautiful woman).[2] The emblem and its verse
adage were inspired by a cut in Andrea Alciati's *Emblematvm Libellvs*
(1534),[3] though the detail of print is unique to the German edition.
Hunger's cut is conspicuous for the absence of a beautiful woman, or
any woman for that matter. Instead, a grotesque skeleton Death has
stalked up to a sleeping Cupid. Leaning over the boy, the skeleton's left
hand grasps a flight of arrows in Cupid's sheath. This, though, is not an
act of theft, as the verse accompaniment makes clear. Death has embarked
on a plan to plant his own deadly arrows in Cupid's quiver; and so, when
it comes for the boy-god to shoot some ripe youth with the arrow of
love, possibly the beautiful woman of the motto, the outcome will be
unexpectedly fatal.

Alongside this idea of death as the scheming and deliberate instigator
of fatality, another species of emblem casts him in a less condemnatory
light. Again inspired by Alciati's work, generations of sixteenth century
emblematists return to the idea of an encounter between skeletal Death

and the boy Cupid in which a few arrows from their respective quivers
are mistakenly switched. Marquale's *Imprese* (1551) offers a picture of
a winged Cupid and a winged Death flying above the mortal world, both
firing down their arrows.[4] Similar, though not identical, cuts appear in
Hunger's *Emblemata* (1542),[5] in Whitney's 1586 text *A Choice of
Emblemes* (*plate 12*),[6] and in Henry Peacham's 1612 edition of *Minerva
Britanna* (*plate 13*).[7] The accounts of the episode vary. Alciati's original
(1534) suggests that both Cupid and Death were blind companions and
during their sojourn together carelessly switched some of their arrows.
Lefèvre's *Emblèmes* (1536) records that after a wine drinking session the
pair drunkenly exchanged weapons.[8] Hunger's 1542 version has Cupid
and Death accidentally interchanging arrows while they were out for a
walk. Daza's *Emblemas* (1549) conjoins tragic possibilities by suggesting
that the arrows were transposed in the darkness of night when the parties
were half asleep.[9] Whitney's Elizabethan version puts the muddle down
to the fact that Death and Cupid spent the night together in an inn and
departed in great haste the following morning, their arrows unwittingly
mingled.

However the error is construed, the consequences are the same, as
here described in the verse accompaniment to Alciati's original print,
titled "De Morte & Amore":

Each has taken the careless weapons of the other:
Death holds the golden ones, Cupid the arrows of bone
Hence an old man who should now be in Hades
Behold, he is in love, and prepares for his pate flowery garlands.
Whereas I, because Cupid with borrowed bow has struck me,
Grow weak, and the Fates are laying their hands on me
Spare me, boy; and you, Death, holding the symbols of victory,
       spare me:
Let me love, make the old man go down to Hades.[10]

Most woodcuts in the emblem books carry a clear and firm moral message,
but the *de morte et amore* cut is unusual in this regard. Neither the
picture nor the verse accompaniment in Alciati's version presents any
kind of lesson from which the reader can learn and adapt his or her life
accordingly. Marquale, Lefèvre, Hunger, Whitney and Peacham all
follow suit, recounting the story of Love and Death but not seeking to
extrapolate moral significances from it. The furthest Alciati ventures is

to have his narrator implore Death to spare his youth, a request founded on hope rather than argument or reason. The point may be that there is no moral message to be derived from this account of one of life's normative, if regrettable, cycles. Rather like destructive storms and other natural disasters, it has to be accepted as part of the procession of mortality. What is implicit in Alciati's emblem is the arbitrary nature of Love and Death, the fact that the individual may be struck without warning and that youth or age can be no foolproof predictor of the consequences. Perhaps the brevity of life in sixteenth century Europe brought into even sharper focus the ephemeral qualities of human life. In times swept by war and plague, the transience of mortality found frightening expression in many facets of artistic endeavor. I recall, particularly, one portraiture in a fifteenth century German manuscript where the realities of premature death are allegorized in a scene recording the baptism of a child.[11] As a monk lowers the infant into the altar font, an emaciated Death stands in the background, towel at the ready to dry him off. In an age where the average life span was less than forty years, emblematists and dramatists alike seemed almost to have felt an obligation to engage and explore the issue of premature death.

Venus' lament in *Venus and Adonis* underscores the unpredictable and inexplicable vagaries of mortality.[12] Why has her beloved and youthful Adonis been taken from her when Death's dart should have slain, rather, the old and infirm? Why should beauty die and feebleness endure?

"If he be dead — O no, it cannot be,
Seeing his beauty, thou shouldst strike at it:
O yes, it may, thou hast no eyes to see,
But hatefully at random dost thou hit.
Thy mark is feeble age, but thy false dart
Mistakes that aim, and cleaves an infant's heart.

"Hadst thou but bid beware, then he had spoke,
And, hearing him, thy power had lost his power.
The Destinies will curse thee for this stroke:
They bid thee crop a weed, thou pluck'st a flower.
Love's golden arrow at him should have fled,
And not Death's ebon dart to strike him dead."
                                        (*Venus and Adonis* 937-48)

A moment earlier she had chided Death as the "Hateful divorce of love" (line 932), and the "Grim-grinning ghost, earth's worm" (line 933). Now she envisages him as the blind ("thou hast no eyes") destroyer of youth when, in fact, his proper target should have been "feeble age." There is no authentic moral underpinning to this argument — except in the suggestion, mooted without warrant, that Death has somehow exceeded his orders — merely the intuitive feel that death is the proper domain of the enfeebled and love the natural prerogative of the young. It is essentially not an ethical argument but an emotive one. With its ebony and golden darts, its dialectic between old age and youth, its balance between grinning Death and "Cupid's bow" (line 581), Shakespeare's *Venus and Adonis* seems to have in mind the familiar emblematic concept of "amor et mors." The lack of a moral foundation to Venus' remonstrations is also reminiscent of the emblem book *topos*.

This said, it is equally evident that Shakespeare is willing to rework the myth to his own ends. It was, of course, not Death who slew the youth in the emblem books of the sixteenth century, but Cupid. The mix-up of arrows had conspired to place some of Death's ebony darts in Cupid's sheath, and some of Cupid's golden darts in Death's quiver. The point is well made in Marlowe's *Tamburlaine, Part 2* where the hero bewails his wife's imminent death, cursing the confusion of arrows that has brought about these tragic consequences:

> Now are those spheres, where Cupid us'd to sit,
> Wounding the world with wonder and with love,
> Sadly supplied with pale and ghastly death,
> Whose darts do pierce the centre of my soul.
>   (II.iv.81-4)[13]

But in Venus' perception of the death of Adonis, she characterizes Death as the deliberate slayer of youth, bewailing the "ebon dart" that has cleft the "infant's heart." The killing of Adonis therefore becomes an act against the orders of the Destinies who have commanded Death to "crop a weed," not a flower. When Venus hears a hunting horn, and the hope springs in her heart that Adonis may yet live, she desperately retracts her censure of Death. She now adds "honors to his hateful name" (line 994) and calls him "king of graves, and grave for kings, / Imperious supreme of all mortal things" (lines 995-6). Her cry is in vain. Death's villainy is without remorse or mercy and the outrage of his murderous action is exacerbated by the suggestion that he has exceeded his authority.

Though Love is countenanced as the victim of Death in Venus' lament, the notion that Love, of itself, was inherently powerful and dangerous was axiomatic in early modern thinking. This is sometimes evidenced even in church settings. The early sixteenth century de la Warr Chantry Chapel at Boxgrove Priory, West Sussex, was built by the de la Warrs as a prospective place of entombment (though, in the event, the Dissolution prevented their burial there) and the implications of the structure are essentially funereal. On the columns and facades of this monument to death, Cupids appear in abundance. Some carry lutes, others flowers, and a few hold hearts carved in the middle of the family crest (*plate 14*). The concatenation of death and love is quite extraordinary. Similarly, in St. Mary's Church at Patrixbourne, Kent, the Pyramus and Thisbe myth is recounted in a late sixteenth century stained glass window (*plate 15*). A distraught Thisbe bewails the sight of a sword-impaled and dying Pyramus while chubby Cupids play with hoops in the panel immediately below.

In Shakespeare's plays images of wounding and pain are constantly linked to Cupidian processes. When Oberon describes Cupid "Flying between the cold moon and the earth" (II.i.156) he says the boy's "love-shaft" looked as if "it should pierce a hundred thousand hearts" (*A Midsummer Night's Dream* II.i.160). Armado, in *Love's Labor's Lost*, drawing on Classical precedent to make the same point, asserts that "Cupid's butt-shaft is too hard for Hercules' club" (I.ii.175-6). It is equally construed as a source of potential fatality — as, for example, in Pandarus' witty and sharply ironic song in *Troilus and Cressida*:

> *Helen.* Let thy song be love. This love will undo us all.
> O Cupid, Cupid, Cupid!
> *Pandarus.* Love? ay, that it shall, i' faith.
> *Paris.* Ay, good now, love, love, nothing but love.
> *Pandarus.* In good troth, it begins so.   [Sings]
> "Love, love, nothing but love, still love, still more!
>   For O, love's bow
>   Shoots buck and doe.
>   The shaft confounds
>   Not that it wounds,
> But tickles still the sore.
> These lovers cry, O ho, they die! . . . ."
>   (III.i.110-21)

Helen's supposition that love will "undo us all," and Pandarus' description of a love that kills, comically prefigure the tragic demise of the attachment between Troilus and Cressida. At its end, the play's hero, hitherto the very flower of courtly love, confronts and kills Diomedes, the rival who usurped his lover's heart, and he does so in the shadows of Troy's doomed walls. The man who once ebulliently commanded Pandarus "From Cupid's shoulder pluck his painted wings, / And fly with me to Cressid!" (III.ii.14-15), in the final gloomy moments of the play has only death and revenge and despair on his lips and mind.

This dual sense of Cupid as a source of enormous power and, concurrently, of mortal danger, is reflected in a range of popular sixteenth century emblems. Central to these is the depiction of Cupid breaking a thunderbolt and thereby signifying the power (and, potentially, destructive power) of love. Alciati offers such a print, titled "Vis Amoris" (the Power of Love), in which a naked child Cupid breaks a bolt of lightening in two (*plate 16*).[14] The theme was reiterated by both Marquale[15] and Hunger, the latter attaching the following explication: "Little Cupid breaks a thunderbolt with his arrow and his fire. This shows that love has such great heat that no power can withstand it. Whether the person be young or old, if the boy is angry he soon makes one into a fool, against which neither power nor cunning can help" (translated from the German).[16] It may be with this idea in mind that Oberon in *A Midsummer Night's Dream* refers to "Cupid's fiery shaft" (II.i.161) and to the point "where the bolt of Cupid fell" (II.i.165). Indeed, an alternative tradition to Love's golden darts, affirmed by Geffrey Whitney's *A Choice of Emblemes*[17] and endorsed by Middleton's *A Chaste Maid in Cheapside* (IV.i.181),[18] talks instead of Love's "fiery darts."

These themes of love's dangers, and potential fatality, are reworked in Guillaume de la Perrière's *Le Theatre des bons engins* (Paris, 1539).[19] Here, in print lxxix, a blindfolded Cupid heats a fire with bellows.[20] The heart in the midst of the fire represents the affections of a lover. Above the fire, in an alchemist's still, the water of tears is being distilled. The verse adage reveals how ardent love often turns to tragedy, and warns the reader "Voyez amour distiller eau de larmes." Mad love, then, can be as much a cause of suffering as it can be of joy. It is an emotion, as the epigram suggests, that has hundreds and thousands of dangers ("des dangers à millier & à cents"). The emblem can be taken on several levels of meaning. There is a religious significance, suggested by the idea of "repentence," and this may imply that one should avoid the foolish acquaintance of love ("Gardons nous dõcq' de sa folle accointãnce") and embrace, rather, the true love of God. The more obvious meaning is that the trials and tribulations of earthly love (that manifested by the devotees of Venus) are both dangerous and unpredictable. It is perhaps this meaning that is evoked in Paris' lament for his lost Juliet in *Romeo and Juliet*:

> *Paris.* Sweet flower, with flowers thy bridal bed I strew —
> O woe, thy canopy is dust and stones! —
> Which with sweet water nightly I will dew,
> Or wanting that, with tears distill'd by moans.
> The obsequies that I for thee will keep
> Nightly shall be to strew thy grave and weep.
> (V.iii.12-17)

The distillation of tears from the sadness of love suggests that in its essence, when love is passed through the figurative alchemist's still, lies grief. A somewhat pessimistic observation but one given at least some experiential credence in plays like *Othello*, *King Lear* and *Romeo and Juliet*.

By far the most arresting conjunction of Love and Death is that drawn explicitly from the *danse macabre*, portraying the union, often the marital union, of a human being to a carrion death. In the theatre this is sometimes expressed violently, as in *The Atheist's Tragedy* where D'Amville's dying words suggest that death has ravished him as he would have ravished the play's heroine, Castabella: "O! the lust of death commits / A rape upon me as I would ha' done / On Castabella" (V.ii.230-2).[21] The emblem books tend to be less lurid, and occasionally present love and death as rather shy and sentimental partners. A 1593 woodcut in Theodore de Bry's *Emblemata*, for example, reveals a faithful lover bringing a rose to his slightly bashful skeletal bride or lover.[22] The motto appended to the print reads "Fui, non svm es, nõ eris," suggesting that escape from the eternal marriage to death is impossible. This sense of certainty, but of a desired certainty, is apparent also in *Edward III*. Audley's imminent death is encapsulated by Prince Edward as a union of love: "Speak thou, that wooest death with thy careless smile / And look'st so merrily upon thy grave, / As if thou were enamor'd on thine end" (IV.ix.21-3).[23] Hans Holbein's *Imagines Mortis* (1545) presented Death as the decimator of human marriage (see *plate 3*).[24] By the 1562 edition, the print has been transformed into a dramatic icon of Death as a marriage partner, with a weeping young bride being led delicately to the grave by her skeletal groom. As he does so, he dances a wedding jig to the music of an obliging lutist. In both cases the prints represent the inconstancy of life. Just as there is love, so there is death; the transience of earthly bonds is bluntly contrasted with the eternal wedlock of death. In the succeeding plate in Holbein's *Imagines Mortis* Death summons a bridegroom who is in the full and fashionable flush of youth, dragging him off by the coat tails and trumpeting what could almost be a rolled-up piece of parchment (his summons?) as he does so. A variation on this theme appears in the Parish Church of St. Mary Magdalene at Newark-on-Trent where an early-Renaissance grinning female Death, her legs splayed in the familiar antic disposition, offers a carnation to the suavely dressed young man in the panel next to her (see *plate 17*). As she does so, she gestures with her other hand to the grave below. A marriage she proposes, sure enough, but the honeymoon suite is a sepulcher.

* * * * *

Kirby Farrell has read *Romeo and Juliet* as an expression of patriarchal structures under stress. In early modern England, he argues, the patriarch symbolically "appropriated the rôle of death himself, subjecting it to human rules."[25] This pattern of death-wielding power he traces to the leading patriarchal figures in Shakespeare's play — the Prince demands obedience "on pain of death" (I.i.103); Old Capulet commands acquiescence or else he will consign his daughter to "hang, beg, starve, die in the streets" (III.v.192). But, equally, it is discernible in the actions of sons or surrogate sons and even servants who "may kill another to identify with the father's strength as warrior hero."[26] A vicious and well-tried order, it is nonetheless an order under threat. Tybalt, for example, tests his surrogate father's authority at the ball, drawing Old Capulet's sharp rebuff "Am I the master here, or you?" (I.v.78); Romeo's rebellious ambitions, too, are flagged, notably in the Chorus' suggestion of a struggle to inherit the rôle of father ("Now old desire doth in his death-bed lie, / And young affection gapes to be his heir" at II.Prol.1-2) and in the young man's self-expressed aspiration to be an emperor (V.i.6-9). At the same time as these internal male challenges are fomenting, another threat to patriarchal authority looms. Farrell suggests that "romance has begun to rival patriarchy as an alternative mode of devotion and deliverance" (p. 134) and the conflict that results makes rebellion unavoidable.

Farrell's thesis embraces, *inter alia*, two central ideas. First, there is the sense of contest between the traditional authoritarians and those who owe loyalty to such people but who must wrestle with deeper and darker motivations. Tybalt's fanaticism, for example, Farrell sees in psychoanalytical terms as "a reaction formation, a means of suppressing one's own taboo impulses by killing off the devilish enemy of authority one might otherwise become" (p. 135). Second, there is the rivalry between the old authoritarian order and romance. But even in opposition, the proponents of romance, Romeo and Juliet, act out patriarchal and Christian forms, and, "Construing love as worship, substituting the beloved for father and God, they seek apotheosis in each other."[27] The pair assert their defiance of patriarchal forms by reconstituting those forms in a manner that seeks to achieve their autonomy. Farrell sees in the culmination of the play the possibility that both Romeo and Juliet, in committing suicide, are driven by the lingering dynamics of patriarchal obligation and control (p. 143).

Though age and authority are often implicitly associated, and love customarily linked with the dalliance of youth, Farrell makes no explicit claim that the play encapsulates a conflict between youth and age. It seems to me that there is here a dimension of the play that could usefully expand Farrell's thesis, and perhaps modify some of the constructions he reads into the part played by Death in the final stages of *Romeo and Juliet*. With this in mind, I propose first to consider the function of Cupid in the early stages of the play and then to move on to look at the *danse macabre* in the latter stages of the work. While it does not seem plausible to argue that the play operates as an explicit theatrical emblem of the *de morte et amore* iconic tradition, I shall suggest that it presents a conflict between youth and age, and one not simply exhibited in the opposition of authority and rebellion but also worked out on the more emblematic level of a conjunction between Love and Death.

Amongst Shakespeare's tragedies, *Romeo and Juliet* is unusual in the frequency of its allusion to Cupid. In a play driven by what Peter Hyland has called "extreme and irrational hatred . . . elevated into a duty,"[28] we might have thought the place of romantic love was limited. Far from it — but even though the theme of love permeates the play, reference to Cupid by name ceases, somewhat peculiarly, after II.v:

> Love's heralds should be thoughts,
> Which ten times faster glides than the sun's beams,
> Driving back shadows over low'ring hills;
> Therefore do nimble-pinion'd doves draw Love,
> And therefore hath the wind-swift Cupid wings.
>   (Juliet, II.v.4-8)

Juliet is waiting impatiently for news from the Nurse about her lover, Romeo. The talk of Cupid's wings mirrors her desire for Love's course to work itself out at a more expeditious pace. In truth, and unbeknown to her, the events preambling tragedy are slipping into place at speed, but they are rather the "shadows over low'ring hills" than the sun's beams. The next time reference is made to Cupid it is not by name but by bawdy inference. Again, Juliet is the speaker:

> Lovers can see to do their amorous rites
> By their own beauties, or, if love be blind,
> It best agrees with night.
>   (III.ii.8-10)

She is, she thinks, about to rendezvous with Romeo. Her thoughts are ribald and bold, focusing on the physicality of mortal love, on the uninhibited contact of amorous and beautiful bodies. In sum, Juliet's words encapsulate the eagerness of youthful sexuality. What she does not and cannot know sitting in her father's orchard is that, during the time that has elapsed between these two cupidinous reveries, the world she inhabits has changed tragically and irreversibly. Mercutio, impeded by Romeo's well-meant but ill-advised intervention, has been slain by Juliet's cousin Tybalt (III.i). And within a few frantic minutes, Tybalt himself has died by the hand of Romeo. While in Juliet's present consciousness the office of youth is a passionate and erotic one, the actuality on Verona's streets is quite different. There, the blood and life of youth have been squandered on the ancient cobble stones. To all of this, Juliet is oblivious, and so she speaks longingly and lustily of blind physical love.[29] Once appraised of the bloody encounters that have paralleled her dreams of love, suspecting first that Romeo has been slain and then discovering that he has killed her cousin, her thoughts never again return to the idea of Cupid. The winged boy disappears without a trace.

This is an extraordinary transformation and, as I shall explain later, I use the word "transformation" deliberately. Cupid's presence in the first half of the play is well-defined. There is talk of Cupid's imponderable "will" at I.i.172; of "Cupid's arrow" at I.i.209; of his blindfold at I.iv.4; of his wings at I.iv.17; of his bow at II.iv.16; and of "Young Adam Cupid's" (II.i.13) propensity for using it. These are all familiar attributes of the boy-god in the prints of Alciati, Held and others. His characteristics are the source of mirth and banter. Mercutio urges the love-struck Romeo to borrow Cupid's wings and soar on high; Romeo declines on grounds that his burden of love is too great:

> *Mercutio.* You are a lover; borrow Cupid's wings,
> And soar with them above a common bound.
>   *Romeo.* I am too sore enpierced with his shaft
> To soar with his light feathers, and so bound
> I cannot bound a pitch above dull woe;
> Under love's heavy burthen do I sink.
>   (I.iv.17-22)

There is an expression of the pain of love here; of the heart "sore enpierced with [Cupid's] shaft." There is also the humor of Mercutio's inference that Romeo so fits the archetype of love-struck youth that he has become a very model of Cupid himself. When Romeo, ecstatic in the presence of his new-found paramour, explains how he surmounted the walls that barriered him from her, he suggests (perhaps recalling Mercutio's earlier comment):

> With love's light wings did I o'erperch these walls,
> For stony limits cannot hold love out,
> And what love can do, that dares love attempt;
> Therefore thy kinsmen are no stop to me.
>   (II.ii.66-9)

All this provides the youth with a nifty conceit with which to impress the young lady but Romeo's hyperbolic diction may also serve to mimic the more serious emblematic oppositions of the play. Here, in a domain controlled by love, Romeo, flitting over a wall with the wings of Love, assumes the persona of Cupid. Later, when Death is preeminent, Romeo rhetorically turns himself into a *danse macabre* figure, threatening in the

manner of skeletal Death to "strew this hungry churchyard" with
Balthazar's limbs, "joint by joint" (V.iii.35). In the extravagant fashion
of an emblem book icon, he maps the mortal journey of the play from
Love to Death, from life to fatality, with caricatured extremity. Certainly,
then, there is greater foreboding in these flying Cupid references than
ever Mercutio or Romeo could guess. Having fashioned Romeo as a
demi-Cupid, soaring above the earth, Mercutio cannot know that Romeo
is as fatal to him as Cupid firing one of Death's "ebon darts." Equally,
Romeo as Cupid is ominously correct in recording that Juliet's kinsmen
will not stop him, a point well attested by the blood that will smear his
sword an act later. And, with telling irony, his own end is comically
prefigured in terms of Cupid imagery. "Alas, poor Romeo, he is already
dead . . . the very pin of his heart cleft with the blind bow-boy's butt-
shaft" (Mercutio at II.iv.13-16). Death is but a short space away.

    None of this surprises us. The opening Prologue had spoken
unambiguously of Romeo and Juliet's "death-mark'd love" (Prologue 9)
and, as we have seen, a tradition of emblematic literature warns audience
and actor alike that Love's machinations are fraught with dangers. The
play makes this point repeatedly, explicitly referring to Cupid as it does
so. Here, for example, is Romeo's explanation as to why the fair Rosaline
will have nothing to do with him:

> she'll not be hit
> With Cupid's arrow, she hath Dian's wit;
> And in strong proof of chastity well arm'd,
> From Love's weak childish bow she lives [unharm'd].
> (I.i.208-11)

Her object is to live "unharm'd" and, in doing so, she follows the advice
of the emblem books; and reminds us a little of Charissa in *The Faerie
Queene* who was "Full of great loue, but *Cupids* wanton snare / As hell
she hated, chast in worke and will" (I.x.30).[30] There the similarity
ends, for Charissa had somehow acquired a daunting brood of children
who were allowed to suckle at will! Even so, she may have operated
along the same pragmatic principles as Rosaline: avoid love; avoid Cupid.
It is a dreary truth but one that Rosaline studiously observes. Her youth
survives.

    The question of Rosaline is an intriguing one. In the Renaissance
portraitures of Cupid and Death, we perceive an intensely masculinized

sense of the power of love and death. This is certainly true of Cupid and Death, who are both standardly flagged as masculine in the texts of the emblem books (and, in the case of Cupid, in the iconography as well). It is also true, to some extent, of their quarries — the men and women who suffer the pains and pleasures of their arrows. In Alciati's original, and in the imitations of Marquale and Whitney, for example, it is old men who have been inadvertently shot with Cupid's arrows and who now thrust their affections on lithesome young females. I have not come across an emblem image of an old woman, shot mistakenly by a golden arrow, trying to wrap her leg lustfully round some passing Adonis. It is men who are the active instigators of matters relating to love and death; women are the passive attendants to this process.

By rejecting love, Rosaline is exercising one of the few possibilities she has for empowerment within such a masculinized ordering of life's affairs. Juliet is less fortunate since the intensity of her love for Romeo apparently renders isolationism untenable. The consequence is an irresistible spiral towards death, marked by her singular lack of control of any of the central elements of that process.   As the play's tragedy begins to unfold in Act II, with Tybalt slaying Mercutio and Romeo slaying Tybalt, Juliet is sitting serenely in an orchard dreaming about love. As the tragedy culminates in Act V, she lies sedated and helpless in the Capulet tomb while a triumvirate of male suitors — Romeo, Paris and "amorous" Death — squabble for possession of her. On awakening, the tragedy is already a *fait accompli*.   In attempting to forestall the tyranny of her father, she has instead succumbed to the ill-judged plan of another male institutional figure, Friar Lawrence. Well meaning, perhaps, the aging cleric is less than the "comfortable friar" (V.iii.148) Juliet supposes him to be when she awakens from her deathly reverie; and he has proved little better in determining her future than her parents had done with their misplaced marriage plans.

The incompatibility of exuberant youth and fallible age is significant in this play. Early in Act I, Shakespeare goes to some lengths to contrapose the two. When old Capulet cries for his sword to fight off a perceived threat, Lady Capulet challenges his call: "A crutch, a crutch! why call you for a sword?" (I.i.76). His behavior and intentions, she implies, are inappropriate for an old man. The trappings and antics of battle do not befit his years; his is the age of infirmity and frailty, of the near-grave, not of youthful action. When Prince Escalus intervenes, he regrets that

> Verona's ancient citizens
> Cast by their grave beseeming ornaments
> To wield old partisans, in hands as old. . . .
>   (I.i.92-4)

Imagistically, the Prince's pun on "grave" places old men like Montague and Capulet in the grave, wielding weapons as old as they are when, in fact, they should carry objects more congenial to their declining years. It is an illuminating comment because, although Prince Escalus has unambiguously banished conflict on Verona's streets, he finds it most reprehensible that old men are engaged in it — suggesting, by default, that such vigorous behavior might be more understandable coming from younger men. This is a peculiarly ageist perspective, as is Lady Capulet's retort twenty lines earlier, and one that heralds the play's disruption of the normative expectations regarding age.

In love, too, there are presumptions about age. Here is Capulet remembering the youthful expeditions of love:

> I have seen the day
> That I have worn a visor and could tell
> A whispering tale in a fair lady's ear. . . .
>   (Capulet I.v.21-3)

There is a degree of friskiness in Capulet's observation but it is a past recollection not a present ambition. The time for wearing a visor and whispering in a fair lady's ear has passed. Romantic love, like war, is the domain of the young. And yet, not too many lines later, as Juliet longs for news of Romeo, she offers a playful exchange:

> *Nurse.* I am a-weary, give me leave a while.
> Fie, how my bones ache! What a jaunce have I!
> *Juliet.* I would thou hadst my bones and I thy news.
>   (II.v.25-7)

When Capulet picked up a sword, his wife was suggesting he was too old to do so, that it was no longer a proper function for him. When the Prince upbraided the warring parties, he argued, similarly, that such activities were incompatible with old age, whose more appropriate rôle was to hover on the edge of the grave. Juliet suggests a transposition of age to youth. To the Nurse's complaint that "my bones ache" she offers the wished for remedy of substitution: "I would thou hadst my bones." The barter is merely a humorous measure of her impatience and exasperation. Even so, it puts down a memorable marker on the journey from the normative patterning of age in age's place and youth in youth's place to a construct where the conditions and aspirations of youth and old age are reversed. Perhaps, rather like Romeo in relation to Cupid and Death, Juliet's image of exchange, of youth for age, of life for death, acts as a rhetorical precursor to the more somber emblems of tragedy at the play's end.

I cannot argue that the detail of Alciati's print "De Morte & Amore," with its winged Cupid firing darts of death and its winged Death firing darts of love, is replicated in the text of *Romeo and Juliet*, for quite clearly it is not. True, all of Cupid's "hits" in this play — Romeo, Juliet, Paris — are dead by the end of it. But equally, there are no rampant old men hotly pursuing the affections of lithesome young women. What there is, though, is a curious imagistic transformation, worked out on various levels, which gradually devolves into a variation on the theme of Cupid and Death. In the first act alone, such transformational images are plentiful.

> Feather of lead, bright smoke, cold fire, sick health,
> Still-waking sleep, that is not what it is!
> (Romeo, I.i.180-1)

> Compare her face with some that I shall show,
> And I will make thee think thy swan a crow.
> (Benvolio, I.ii.86-7)

> If he be married,
> My grave is like to be my wedding-bed.
> (Juliet, I.v.134-5)

These utterances, and others of their ilk, attest to the transformational proclivities of the play from its very beginnings. In fact, they go beyond simple transformation; they are images of contrariety, of antithesis. The feather is the opposite of lead; the white swan the opposite of the black crow; the barren grave the opposite of the fertile wedding bed. Commensurate with the sense of foreboding established by the opening prologue, there is the repeated insinuation that the norms of mortality are threatened with reversal.

In this regard, Juliet's speculation that if Romeo is married then her grave "is like to be my wedding-bed" (I.v.135) is disturbing. For one in the full flush of youth, it is an odd prophesy, perhaps attributable to the extravagant hyperbole of teenage love. Nonetheless, she reiterates the claim on several occasions. For her, marriage to death becomes the logical and expedient alternative to earthly marriage:

> O sweet my mother, cast me not away!
> Delay this marriage for a month, a week,
> Or, if you do not, make the bridal bed
> In that dim monument where Tybalt lies.
>   (III.v.198-201)

> I'll to my wedding-bed,
> And death, not Romeo, take my maiden-head!
>   (III.ii.136-7)

> Or hide me nightly in a charnel-house,
> O'ercover'd quite with dead men's rattling bones,
> With reeky shanks and yellow chapless skulls;
> Or bid me go into a new-made grave,
> And hide me with a dead man in his shroud —
>   (IV.i.81-5)

Iconographically, Holbein's representation of "The Bride" seems most relevant to these allusions. Yet, while Holbein's bride accompanies Death somewhat reluctantly to the grave, Juliet judges the prospect of a carrion union as distinctly alluring when the alternative is not to be with her Romeo. In the third quotation, her allusion to the charnel house and grave, reflecting her wish to be covered with dead men's rattling bones or to be hidden with a dead man in his shroud, does not expressly mention marriage, though emblematically it seems reasonable to suggest that this is the inference — and Juliet is quite specific that it is a dead *man* with whom she envisages herself covered or wrapped![31]

If the first half of Romeo and Juliet broadly follows the iconographic traditions of Cupid, then the second half falls very much within the domain of the *danse macabre*. That theme is reiterated not only by Juliet but by several other characters in relation to her death. Both Capulet and

Paris, assuming Juliet is dead in Act IV, articulate her mortality in terms
of a repulsive marriage to Death:

> O son, the night before thy wedding-day
> Hath Death lain with thy wife. There she lies,
> Flower as she was, deflowered by him.
> Death is my son-in-law, Death is my heir,
> My daughter he hath wedded. I will die,
> And leave him all; life, living, all is Death's.
>   (Capulet to Paris, IV.v.35-40)

> Beguil'd, divorced, wronged, spited, slain!
> Most detestable Death, by the beguil'd,
> By cruel cruel thee quite overthrown!
> O love, O life! not life, but love in death!
>   (Paris, IV.v.55-8)

Their sense of loss contrasts forcefully with Juliet's sense of gain. Capulet
inverts the normal reproductive cycles of marriage into a grotesque new
sexuality. Picking up his earlier idea that Death "lies on" Juliet like an
untimely frost, Capulet restates and develops the image, suggesting that
Death has "lain with thy [Paris'] wife" and that she has been "deflowered
by him." The plucking of flowers suggested in the Cupid emblems of
Alciati and others as a symbol of love's power is here transposed into a
symbol of Death's power. It is perhaps indicative of the movement in
the play from love to fatality, from Cupid to Death, that Capulet goes on
to suggest that "Our bridal flowers serve for a buried corse" (IV.v.89);
that a grief-stricken Paris arrives at the Capulet tomb and promises Juliet
"Sweet flower, with flowers thy bridal bed I strew"; and that in the final
moments of the play, as in no other Shakespearean tragedy, the stage is
strewn with flowers.

What of Romeo in all of this? Murray Levith suggests in his time
away from Verona, Romeo has "grown up."[32] If there has been, as
Levith puts it, "maturation in Mantua" (p. 60), it isn't entirely certain
what *kind* of maturation this has been. Post-Mantua Romeo seems to be
almost Pistol-like in his braggardliness, advising Balthazar that he is
more "fierce and inexorable" than "empty tigers or the roaring sea"
(V.iii.38-9). He soon shows, though, that this is more than mere rhetoric
when, having encountered Paris, who has just strewn the tomb with
flowers, he gives him one chance to leave and, this refused, kills him.

He seems almost to have transposed himself into a cavorting Death-figure, not entirely void of emotion or compassion, but certainly assured of his power and single-minded in his purpose. But then, even the pre-Mantua Romeo was apt to sensationalize Death, describing it as "love-devouring death" in Act II. At last, as he breaks open the Capulet tomb in the third scene of Act V, he revels in the hyperbolized symbolism of his actions:

> Thou detestable maw, thou womb of death,
> Gorg'd with the dearest morsel of the earth,
> Thus I enforce thy rotten jaws to open,
> And in despite I'll cram thee with more food.
> > [*Romeo begins to open the tomb.*]
> > (V.iii.45-7)

Ordinarily, the "maw" is the craw or stomach of an animal.[33] We get some glimpses of devouring-hell's "maw" in the extraordinary Doom murals at the Church of St. Lawrence at Combe and at the Church of St. James the Great at South Leigh, both in Oxfordshire, and at the Church of St. Thomas, at Salisbury in Wiltshire. The first two of these lie on the direct route from Stratford-on-Avon to London. In all three instances, demons drive the damned into the devouring jaws and belly of a gigantic fish, a hell-monster — a beast recorded in Spenser's *The Faerie Queene* when he talks of "The dreadfull Fish, that hath deseru'd the name / Of Death, and like him lookes in dreadfull hew" (II.xii.24). In each of the church murals, the maw of Death is contrasted with the joys of heaven and the beatific presence. At the Church of St. Thomas, for example, those about to be devoured by the hell-fish look across in hopeless regret at the fortunate few who, on the other side of the chancel, raise their hands in joy at the prospect of heavenly reward. At South Leigh, God welcomes the saved into the beauteous domain of heaven while, again on the right side of the chancel, a thronging mass of lassoed miscreants is dragged and prodded towards the jaws and maw of the same beast.

Romeo's idea of death is not one that embraces a duplicity of heaven and hell. Death, for him, is simply hell — as it is for others who allude to it in what on the surface appears to be one of Shakespeare's most Christianized of plays. In fact, Romeo's sense of the afterlife owes more to the Classical notions of the underworld than it does to a Biblical scheme of loss and salvation. This may be partly explained by the idea, implied already, that Romeo actually enjoys the archetypal pattern of the mortal battling the immortal (a paradigm that recurs frequently, of course, in Graeco-Roman myth) or even the Herculean notion of the mortal acquiring the accoutrements of immortality. For example, a few lines before the "maw" reference he had actually assumed for himself the spectral mantle of a prancing devouring Death, warning his servant, Balthazar, to leave or else "I will tear thee joint by joint, / And strew this hungry churchyard with thy limbs" (V.iii.35-6). There is, for me, something almost comic about this, perhaps because I find it reminiscent of Furnace's absurd inference that the gluttonous Justice Greedy in Massinger's *A New Way To Pay Old Debts* is a kind of Death figure whose "stomach's as insatiate as the grave" (I.ii.47).[34] Romeo surely does not intend his allusion to be humorous but the enthusiasm of his rhetoric suggests, at least, that he relishes his potential rôle as limb-strewing Death in a "hungry" churchyard; and certainly you might have supposed that a firm dismissal, without the somewhat excessive threat of dismemberment, would have been sufficient to discharge most people from a graveyard at midnight, let alone your servant. Then, having slain Paris, his second killing in the play, Romeo drags his foe's body with heavy symbolism into the "maw" of the devouring tomb. Dumping Paris in the tomb, he reverts, in variation, to the idea that he is, himself, "Death" — but suggests, as well, that he is also the conqueror of Death. Looking upon the body of Paris, he commands "Death, lie thou there, by a dead man interr'd" (V.iii.87).

Aside from Romeo's personal dispositions, though, the implicit disavowal of a Hebraic scheme of heaven and hell resonates strongly with the iconography of "Cupid and Death" in the emblem books. Here, too, there is no sense of heaven and hell but, rather, a very clear antithesis between Love who hovers, bow at the ready, in the left hand corner of most prints, and Death who hovers in the right hand corner. The confusion of arrows may, indeed, have been a simple and honest mistake (as suggested by Alciati and Whitney, for example) but the point is that it *is* a mistake and that the two figures in question, Love and Death, operate in separate spheres and to very different agendas. The purpose of the emblem books is to explain one or two of life's accidental mysteries: why young people sometimes die; and why old people are sometimes consumed by romantic friskiness. That is all. There is no concern with the evolution of the story or the emblem outside that point into, for example, the tradition of the *memento mori* or Biblical eschatology. *Romeo and Juliet*, on the other hand, moves beyond the emblem book perimeters into a more ambiguous and complicated iconic domain. The "Cupid and Death" anecdote is certainly present, but it becomes conflated, as well, with *danse macabre* traditions.

We see this most obviously in the persona of Romeo, whose disposition flits between the extremities of Cupid's victim and of devouring Death itself. In the final moments of the play, he presents yet another possibility. When, at last, he looks upon Juliet, supposing that she is dead, his thoughts move away from the rhetoric of Death the devourer, and from a personification of himself as the same, into a different topography of iconographic symbolism. No longer Death or Death's conqueror, Romeo becomes Death's rival for the affections of Juliet. He draws on that same tradition of marriage and death to which Juliet herself has given prominence:

> Shall I believe
> That unsubstantial Death is amorous,
> And that the lean abhorred monster keeps
> Thee here in dark to be his paramour?
> For fear of that, I still will stay with thee,
> And never from this palace of dim night
> Depart again.
>
> (V.iii.102-8)

Death is still a monstrosity, but no longer a devouring monstrosity. Death is now "amorous" Death, a skeletal ("unsubstantial") kidnapper who has snatched and incarcerated the woman he loves. The love rivalry of the play then, the triangular interplay among Romeo and Juliet and Paris, is now reworked with deformed resonances. Old Death has become the third and final suitor to the affections of Juliet, the ultimate victor in the marital contest, hideously triumphant over the warmth and brightness of youth. In order to claim his bride, Romeo, too, must die.[35]

There is, however, no obvious sense of celebration in Romeo's undertaking to remain with his beloved Juliet in the dark palace of the grave. Perhaps for this reason, Roland Wymer has concluded the play offers "virtually no reference to a future paradise of lovers in which they [Romeo and Juliet] will be reunited."[36] True, the state of death in *Romeo and Juliet* is hardly to be construed as paradisial. Even so, it is an escape from the miasma of earthly existence and Juliet's allusion to marriage with Death consistently emphasizes death as a sanctuary, as a condition to which she can flee to escape the pangs of mortal life. To others, though, her marriage with Death, and the death of so many young people in the play, are stark symbols of untimeliness. This theme can be traced to the early scenes of the play, where Romeo has his own ominous premonition "of untimely death" (I.iv.111). Thereafter, Benvolio laments that the slain Mercutio's spirit has left the earth "too untimely" (III.i.118); Capulet, looking down at his daughter's body, bewails that "Death lies on her like an untimely frost" (IV.v.28); Tybalt's "untimely death" (V.iii.234) is remembered by Friar Lawrence, who goes on to recall that when he entered the tomb he saw, to his consternation, that the unfortunate Paris and Romeo there "untimely lay" (V.iii.258). The sense that youth and age are juxtaposed, and their normative situations reversed, comes out strongly in the final image of the play. The concluding visual spectacle presents youth dead and old age living. Romeo, Paris, and Juliet lie lifeless, and young Tybalt rests within view, his "green" corpse "fest'ring in his shroud" (IV.iii.42-3). Those, their relatives, who remain alive clamor around them: old Capulet, old Lady Capulet, old Montague. In a final emblematic irony, the aging representatives of familial tyranny, the ones for whom the grave ought to have beckoned, stand together, alive and well, mourning the passing of youth.

* * * * *

What, then, does all this signify? Patricia Carlin sees the denouement of the play in triumphal terms.[37] Like its Medieval antecedents, Shakespeare's theatre understands that in order to overcome death it must be confronted. This, Carlin suggests, is the starting point for all Shakespearean tragedy but, in the case of *Romeo and Juliet*, the dramatist takes the idea a step forward in enacting the process itself (p. 202). In the final act of *Romeo and Juliet* the "links between married love and death reach their ultimate intensity, culminating in the scene of the lovers' deaths where, at the level of both action and language, the act of love and the act of suicide, sexual union in marriage and union in death, become completely and finally, indistinguishable" (p. 192). Carlin identifies some of the transformational imagery of the play — especially Capulet's speech culminating with "Our bridal flowers serve for a buried corse" at IV.v.89 — as early evidence of this union. The problem is, though, that the words of Capulet are hardly persuasive on this matter. He is not, of course, talking about Juliet's marriage to Romeo but about her proposed marriage to Paris. Further, and perhaps more importantly, the play does not *feel* triumphant at its end, and I certainly detect little comfort for Juliet. Be she married to Romeo or Death or whoever, she remains no more than a pawn in the ordering of the world and the afterworld. The point is surely not that Death and Love have been harmonized but that, in that cruel and tragic twist of fate so implicit in the emblematic representations of *de morte et amore*, the lives of beautiful youth are mourned rather than celebrated and that the flowers which should have bedecked their wedding festival now bestrew their graves.

Kirby Farrell's reading of the play's end is intriguing. He sees in the final movements a migration of patriarchal structures from their normative Capulet versus Montague matrices. Romeo's surrender of life in order to rescue Juliet from the monster Death is perceived as a reassertion of "the warrior's debt of the son to his father" (p. 144). And by taking his own life and descending into the underworld, Romeo "gives sublime new life — eschatological life — to Verona's feud" (p. 145). Attractive as this argument may seem, it relies heavily on what Romeo says and, as we have seen, Romeo is quite a talker. It is one thing to challenge Death to battle, as Romeo does, but what does this *actually* mean? Not very much, I would suggest, and I suspect the Elizabethans would have concurred. As Llewellyn, Morris, Frye and others have demonstrated, an important purpose of the *memento mori* tradition was to show that Death was both invulnerable and unavoidable. A plethora of iconographers from Holbein to Peacham represent Death as the insuperable conqueror, and the idea that he could be overcome through confrontation or somehow engaged in an extended feud-like conflict did not loom large in sixteenth century thinking. Certainly, there was a belief in the efficacy of contemplating the inevitability of death, but as an encouragement to comprehending the full consequences of mortality rather than as a means of defeating Death.

In interpreting the closing moments of *Romeo and Juliet*, the emblem books may be instructive. The "De Morte & Amore" *topos* is interesting and unusual in the nature of its moral import. As noted earlier in this chapter, it appears to have none. Most emblems, indeed the vast majority of emblems, offer some moral aphorism or other. That, after all, was the purpose of the genre — to educate and enlighten. But the *de morte et amore* emblems, in their numerous variations, can do neither. All they are able to offer is a statement of two unavoidable features of the world:

sometimes young folk die young, and sometimes old people succumb to romantic adventurism. It is never an exhortation to action, simply an observation. Romantic adventurism may be lacking amongst the senior citizens of *Romeo and Juliet* but, equally, there is no shortage of young people dying. Perhaps the play's full tragedy is that there is no explanation for all this, and that in every age and place Romeos and Juliets and Mercutios and Tybalts and Parises will die in the flower of their youth. And perhaps the flowers that lie strewn across the stage at play's end regret not only the unfathomable passing of these young people but of those who have perished in the past and of those who will do so in the future.

The assertion that love and death can lead to youthful fatality may seem a rather unremarkable objective for a play, but it needs to be reviewed in light of Farrell's notion of the death-wielding patriarch. The patterning of Verona's authoritarian structures has apotheosized its leaders, customizing them as the arbiters of life or death. When Escalus, the Prince of Verona, banishes Romeo, notice how the young man frames the judgment:

> There is no world without Verona walls,
> But purgatory, torture, hell itself.
> Hence "banished" is banish'd from the world,
> And world's exile is death. . . .
>
> (III.iii.17-20)

This, he would have us believe, is the judgment of deity that has been passed upon him — a condemnation to purgatory, to hell, to death itself — and, as prone to hyperbole as Romeo may be, the rhetoric here, as elsewhere, purports to transform mere mortals into something more than they are. The lesson of the play, a *memento mori* lesson perhaps, may be that attempts to impose a god-like order on the world can function for a time but are inevitably reduced to absurdity when the real powers (whatever they be) that inform and direct human affairs intervene. Despite Romeo's claims, Verona is not the beginning and the end of the cosmos; and its rulers are less than gods. The deaths of young people in this play confirm a universe that ultimately moves beyond human control and comprehension. That truth is neither an automatic cue for celebration nor a necessary cause of regret; it is merely factual.

Notes

1. Edgar Wind's "Amor as a God of Death" in *Pagan Mysteries in the Renaissance*, Revised Ed. (Oxford: Oxford University Press, 1980), pp. 152-70, remains one of the best discussions of the broad ideas relating to the relationship of Love and Death. Important, too, is Denis de Rougemont's seminal "The Love of Death," in *Love in the Western World*, trans. Montgomery Belgion (New York: Pantheon, 1956), pp. 42-6. Horst W. Janson examines visual images of Love and Death in "A 'Memento Mori' among early Italian Prints," *Journal of the Warburg and Cortauld Institutes*, 3 (1939-40), pp. 243-8. Samuel C. Chew explores iconographic representations of Love and Death in *The Pilgrimage of Life* (1962; reprint ed., Port Washington: Kennikat Press, 1973), pp. 190-2. Judith Dundas has offered a valuable discussion of Cupid and Death iconographies in her essay "The Masks of Cupid and Death," *Comparative Drama*, 29 (1995), 38-60.

2. Wolfgang Hunger, *Emblemata* (Paris: Christian Wechel, 1542), "Das absterben einer schoenen frawen" (emblem LXVI).

3. Alciati, *Emblematvm Libellvs* (Christian Wechel, 1534).

4. Giovanni Marquale, *Imprese* (Lyon: Bonhomme, 1551), "Della morte e d'Amore" (emblem 137).

5. Hunger, "Von dem Tod, vnd der Lieb" (emblem LXV)

6. Geffrey Whitney, *A Choice of Emblemes*, "De morte, et amore: Iocosum," p. 132. Judith Dundas suggests that "Iocosum" (= humorous) relates to "the accidental meeting of Cupid and Death at an inn and the havoc that results" (p. 45).

7. Henry Peacham, *Minerva Britanna* (London: W. A. Dight, 1612), "De Morte, et Cupidne," p. 172.

8. Jehan Lefèvre, *Emblèmes* (Paris: Wechel, 1536), "Contre la Mort hastive" (emblem 112).

9. Bernardino Daza, *Emblemas* (Lyon: Bonhomme, 1549), "De la que murio antes de tiempo" (emblem 66).

10. The translation here is provided in *Andreas Alciatus. 1: The Latin Emblems, Indexes and Lists*, ed. Peter M. Daly, with Virginia W. Callahan and assisted by Simon Cuttler (Toronto: University of Toronto Press, 1985), emblem 155.

11. "Death at the Baptism," in the Warder Collection, New York. The print is reproduced in Robert E. Lerner, Standish Meacham, and Edward McNall Burns, *Western Civilizations: Their History and Their Culture*, 12th ed. (New York and London: W. W. Norton, 1993), p. 359.

12. Shakespeare's treatment of love and death has been broached in a variety of works. Among the most extensive and illuminating of these is Norman Rabkin's exploration of the idea of Eros and Death in *Shakespeare and the*

Common Understanding (New York: Free Press, 1967), pp. 150-91.
Important, also, are: H. A. Mason, *Shakespeare's Tragedies of Love* (New
York: Barnes and Noble, 1970), pp. 42-5; Roger Stilling, *Love and Death
in Renaissance Tragedy* (Baton Rouge: Louisiana State University Press,
1976), pp. 67-81; Theodore Spencer, *Death in Elizabethan Tragedy: A
Study of Convention and Opinion in the Elizabethan Drama* (1936; reprint
ed., New York: Pageant Books, 1960). More recent works include: James
L. Calderwood's discussion of sex and death in *Shakespeare and the Denial
of Death* (Amherst: University of Massachusetts Press, 1987), pp. 46-76;
Kirby Farrell's consideration of Love and Death in *Romeo and Juliet* in
Play, Death, and Heroism in Shakespeare (Chapel Hill: The University of
North Carolina Press, 1989), pp. 131-47. Peggy Muñoz Simonds, focusing
on *Cymbeline*, has offered a scholarly analysis of later Florentine ideas
relating to Psyche, Cupid and Death, (p. 83 et seq.) in *Myth, Emblem, and
Music in Shakespeare's Cymbeline: An Iconographic Reconstruction*
(Newark: University of Delaware Press, 1992). Patricia L. Carlin has
commented extensively on sexuality and death in relation to *Love's Labor's
Lost* (pp. 111-41 ff.) and *Romeo and Juliet* (pp. 151-218) in *Shakespeare's
Mortal Men: Overcoming Death in History, Comedy and Tragedy* (New
York: Peter Lang, 1993); Michael Neill has written on the relationship
between death and the erotic in *Antony and Cleopatra* in *Issues of Death:
Mortality and Identity in English Renaissance Tragedy* (Oxford: Clarendon
Press, 1997), pp. 319-20.
13. Christopher Marlowe, *The Complete Plays*, ed. J. B. Steane (Harmonds-
    worth: Penguin Books, 1973).
14. Alciati, *Emblemi di Andrea Alciato* (Padua: 1626), "Vis Amoris" (emblem
    108).
15. Marquale, "Forza d'Amore" (emblem 95).
16. Hunger, "Krafft der Lieb" (emblem LXXIII). The translation here is
    provided in *Andreas Alciatus. 2: Emblems in Translation: Index Emblem-
    aticus*, ed. Peter M. Daly, assisted by Simon Cuttler. (Toronto: University
    of Toronto Press, 1985).
17. Geffrey Whitney, *A Choice of Emblemes* (Leyden: Christopher Plantin,
    1586), "De morte, et amore: Iocosum," p. 132.
18. Thomas Middleton, *A Chaste Maid in Cheapside*, ed. Alan Brissenden
    (London: Ernest Benn, 1974).
19. Guillaume de la Perrière, *Le Theatre des bons engins* (Paris: 1539), print
    lxxix.
20. The print is reproduced, with commentary, in Charles Moseley's *A Century
    of Emblems* (Aldershot: Scolar Press, 1989), p. 53.
21. Cyril Tourneur, *The Atheist's Tragedy* in *John Webster and Cyril Tourneur:
    Four Plays*, ed. John Addington Symonds (New York: Hill and Wang,
    1966).

22. Theodore de Bry, *Emblemata* (Frankfurt am Main: 1593), "Fui, non svm es, nō eris" (no pagination).

23. The version used is that in G. Blakemore Evans et al., eds., *The Riverside Shakespeare*, 2nd Ed. (Boston: Houghton Mifflin, 1997).

24. Hans Holbein, *Imagines Mortis* (1538 first publ.; Lyon: 1545), sig. C4r.

25. Farrell, p. 133.

26. Farrell, p. 137.

27. Farrell, p. 137.

28. Peter Hyland, *An Introduction to Shakespeare* (New York: St. Martin's Press, 1996), p. 191.

29. Charles A. Hallett and Elaine S. Hallett, *Analyzing Shakespeare's Action: Scene versus Sequence* (Cambridge: Cambridge University Press, 1991), p. 60, have offered valuable insights into the sequence in which information is imparted to Juliet at this point in the play, and elsewhere.

30. Edmund Spenser, *The Faerie Queene*, ed. Thomas P. Roche (Harmondsworth: Penguin Books, 1978).

31. There may be something more to this last quotation (IV.i.81-5, above). A print titled "Impar coniugium" in Geffrey Whitney's *A Choice of Emblemes* (1586), p. 99, recalls the practice of the vile tyrant Mezentius who devised the unusual punishment of tying those who displeased him to the bodies of plague victims. There the unfortunates languished until they contracted the disease and themselves died. Whitney departs from the text of his source (Virgil's *Aeneid*) to offer the following moral paradigm (page 99):

Those wedding webbes, which some doe weaue with ruthe,
As when the one, with straunge disease doth pine:
Or when as age, bee coupled vnto youthe,
And those that hate, inforced are to ioyne,
    This representes: and doth those parentes showe,
    Are tyrauntes meere, who ioyne their children soe

    . . . .

    But parentes harde, that matches make for goodes:
    Can not be free, from guilte of childrens bloodes.

The issue of plague, then, is tied in with ill-fated marriage. *Romeo and Juliet* is riddled with plague allusions. The dying Mercutio three times wishes "A plague o' both your houses" (III.i.91, 99-100, 106); and the letter that would have saved the star-crossed lovers is delayed because the deliverer, Friar John, is quarantined in a house where "the infectious pestilence did reign" (V.ii.10). But, if there is an emblematic echo in Shakespeare's text of Whitney's marital moral, then it is a gentle echo. A different emblematic tradition dominates the conclusion of the play: that of the dance of death.

32. Murray J. Levith, *Shakespeare's Italian Settings and Plays* (New York: St. Martin's Press, 1989), p. 60.

33. See "maw" in the *Oxford English Dictionary*, 2nd Ed.: "The stomach (of men and animals); the cavity of the stomach." Shakespeare uses a similar sense of maw in *Macbeth* where Macbeth, speaking to Banquo's ghost, observes "If charnel-houses and our graves must send / Those that we bury back, our monuments / Shall be the maws of kites" (III.iv.70-2). The *OED* records numerous Medieval and Renaissance precedents.

34. Philip Massinger, *A New Way To Pay Old Debts* in *Four Jacobean City Comedies*, ed. Gamini Salgado (Harmondsworth: Penguin Books, 1985).

35. Dundas, p. 42.

36. Roland Wymer, *Suicide and Despair in the Jacobean Drama* (Brighton, England: The Harvester Press, 1986), p. 117.

37. Carlin, pp. 151-218.

Chapter 5

౪ల ౧ఞ

Hamlet and the Death's Head

More than 800 years ago, a Benedictine monk, Heinrich von Melk, wrote a satirical poem titled "Von des tôdes gehügede" (c. 1150-60; "Remembrance of Death" or "Memento Mori"). The Austrian society he saw around him, with its corrupted morals and distasteful courtly ways, is the subject of a series of stinging rebukes. Von Melk was not the first to use the idea of *memento mori* but his emphasis on the dangers of unbridled pleasure and of the need to remember the certainty of death signals a common theme in the later Middle Ages and Renaissance. Five centuries later, Giovanni Martinelli's painting "Memento Mori" (1625) shows Death approaching a group of banqueters.[1] The ingredients of a fleshy, excessive life are abundantly evident: sumptuous food, the rich courtierly habiliments, a canoodling couple in the center-back of the painting. Equally apparent is the shock of the debauchers at the arrival of this unwelcome guest. The symbolism of the painting is intended as a reminder to the living of the ephemeral nature of human life and of the inherent futility of mortal vanities. Remember death, the painting warns its viewer, and adjust your life accordingly.

Iconographically, Martinelli's painting is in the tradition of the dance of death — an animated skeleton Death intrudes rather smugly and unexpectedly on human activity. The theme of *memento mori* could occur in any artistic genre but its visual presentation through Hans Holbein's dance of death series (1532-62) was preeminent. There were, of course, other icons of mortality: notably, the death's head (see *plates 2, 4,* and *8*), consisting simply of a skull, sometimes depicted with bones; and what may be called a "static corpse," by which I mean representation of skeletal death as an inanimate cadaver which is wholly or mostly unfleshed.

Of this last iconographic species of *memento mori*, numerous Medieval and Renaissance English examples remain extant today — some of which have already been mentioned. William E. Engel has argued that the admonition in the early modern period to remember what is to come (that is, death and an afterlife) "involves a projection of a series of linked images of oneself in various states of decay, dissolution, and disintegration, and then — depending on one's religious upbringing coupled with the liberties and limits of one's individual, mortal imaginings — some transfigured image of oneself in the afterlife."[2] A good illustration of this projection of personal physical deterioration is the late fifteenth century cadaver effigy on the tomb of Abbot Wakeman in Tewkesbury Abbey, Gloucestershire, which portrays the cleric as a skeletonized body, mere skin and bone, with stone worms and vermin crawling through his body (*plate 10*). There are similar skeletal alabaster figures in Salisbury Cathedral[3]; and a remarkable *transi* in Canterbury Cathedral in which the fifteenth century effigy of Archbishop Henry Chichele, founder of All-Souls College and the man who *actually* put forward the Salic Law argument to Henry V, is shadowed by a skeletonized marble cadaver in an arched casket a few feet beneath. It is a chilling and apposite reminder of mortality. The lesson in each case is a simple one, condensed neatly by Horatio in *The Spanish Tragedy* as he remembers the death of Andrea. To Bel-Imperia's question "was Don Andrea's carcase lost?" he responds that he had retrieved the cadaver, even attempted to revive it,

> But neither friendly sorrow, sighs nor tears
> Could win pale Death from his usurped right.
> (I.iv.38-9)[4]

Death's right to claim human life is usurped since, before the Fall of Man, no such right existed. Death held no sway in the lives of Adam and Eve until their violation empowered him.

Another interesting iconic example occurs in St. Alban's Cathedral, Hertfordshire, where the former students of one John Thomas Hylocomius, a teacher and headmaster from the continent who died in January 1595, celebrate the contribution he made to their lives. In a lengthy Latin poem written large and high on the south aisle wall of the abbey, former pupil John Westerman sings the praises of Hylocomius (his learning, his skills as a teacher, his leadership), suggesting that although his former master is now no more than a "mere shade" his inspiration and fine scholarly reputation live on. At the bottom of the poem, a prostrate skeletal Death acts as a sober reminder of mortality, a condition pervasive to all living things — even the learned Hylocomius — and a pair of skulls and cross-bones, one either side of the skeleton, give further emphasis to this point (*plate 18*). This funereal celebration, then, combines several *memento mori*: the poem itself, which iterates textually the certainties of mortality; the icon of the skeleton; and the image of the skull and cross-bones (essentially, the death's head). It is on the last of these, the death's head, that I would like to focus my initial discussion.

Roland Mushat Frye draws a parallel between Hamlet's contemplation of Yorick's skull and Frans Hals' celebrated oil painting *A Young Man with a Skull*, noting that "where we might anticipate a mood of anxiety, Hals shows that the face and indeed the whole posture reflect security, ease, even serenity. In the age of Shakespeare and Hals, that was the result expected from a serious contemplation upon death."[5] This is somewhat at odds with our contemporary sensibilities which tend to regard the image of the skull with some repugnance, and it certainly undermines what Frye calls the "Flaccid twentieth-century assumption that Shakespeare's prince was uniquely morbid in the comments he makes in the graveyard at Elsinore" (p. 291). Elsewhere, too, Shakespeare shows himself attracted to the power of the skull as an image. The Friar in *Romeo and Juliet* refers forbiddingly to "eyeless skulls" (V.iii.126) in the Capulet monument. In *Richard III*, Clarence recounts a macabre dream in which the skulls and bones of the dead lay scattered at the bottom of the sea, with countless riches of gold ingots and jewels resting in the skullcaps and protruding through the eye sockets "As 'twere in scorn of eyes" (I.iv.31). Of no use to the dead are the treasures of the mortal world. A death's head is cursed in *The Merchant of Venice* when Morocco chooses the wrong casket and the scroll advising his failure is rolled up in the eye socket of a skull; and Portia, recollecting the familiar accompaniment of the cross-bones, insists that she would "rather be married to a death's-head with a bone in his mouth" (I.ii.50-2) than to either of her first two suitors.

Shakespeare would have learnt about the death's head as a child from any number of gravestones; and as a motif it would have been commonplace in both religious and secular contexts. Nigel Llewellyn has noted that the death's head skull "appears on even modest domestic paraphernalia, including spoons and snuff-boxes"[6] and Frye has recorded the prevalence of death's head objects in sixteenth century everyday culture, ranging from miniature ivory skulls to skull-shaped watches.[7] Many churches and cathedrals, as is the case of Gloucester Cathedral, for example, conspired to represent a skull or hourglass, or both, at a point close to the main entrance portal.[8] Equally, it was a popular theme in secular public places, a good illustration being the death's head clock carved by Spanish prisoners after the débâcle of the Spanish Armada in 1588 and housed in the White Bear Inn (now called the Red Lion Hotel), a Medieval ale house in Salisbury, Wiltshire (*plate 4*).[9]

In later years, Shakespeare might have viewed and read about it in numerous emblem books, as, for example, in Paradin's *Heroicall Devises*[10] or Simeoni's *Pvrtratvres Or Emblemes*, both published in London in 1591 (see *plate 21*).[11] Geffrey Whitney's 1586 print "ex maximo minimum," revealing a skull and bone, summarized what was one of the most common emblematic themes of the sixteenth century:

> Where liuely once, Gods image was expreste,
> Wherein, sometime was sacred reason plac'de,
> The head, I meane, that is so ritchly bleste.
> With sighte, with smell, with hearinge, and with taste.
> Lo, nowe a skull, both rotten, bare, and drye,
> A relike meete in charnell house to lye.[12]

The physical being, Whitney warns us, with all its wonderful faculties is still reduced to a bare, rotten, dry skull, a "relike meete in charnell house to lye." This theme is common enough in Elizabethan and Jacobean drama. In Tourneur's *The Atheist's Tragedy*, for instance, there is an inventive play on the significances of the death's head. In a bid to escape from his pursuers, Charlemont hides in a charnel house (a building where human bones were stored in a churchyard), and climbing in amongst the bones he leans against a death's head for support and falls when it gives way:

I'll hide me here i' th' charnel house,
This convocation-house of dead men's skulls.
> [*In getting into the charnel house he takes hold of
> a death's head; it slips, and he staggers.*]
Death's head, deceivest my hold?
Such is the trust to all mortality.

(IV.iii.77-80)[13]

The death's head icon is here theatrically emblematized, precipitating an accident which suggests itself as an animated *memento mori*, a physical illustration before our very eyes of the fragility and unreliability of mortal things. Later in the same scene, this idea is developed and extended with the distracted D'Amville entering the charnel house and railing against a death's head he accuses of staring at him; and with Charlemont and Castabella lying down to sleep, each with a death's head for a pillow — a gesture reminding us of Archbishop Chichele's shadow cadaver, of life mirrored by death in a transient mortal state.

A process not entirely dissimilar, but considerably more comic, occurs when Falstaff lampoons Bardolph's red face, suggesting that in reminding him of a death's head it is of great spiritual value:

> *Falstaff.*   I make as good use of it as
> many a man doth of a death's-head or a *memento
> mori*. I never see thy face but I think upon hell-fire
> and Dives that lived in purple; for there he is in his
> robes, burning, burning.

(*1 Henry IV* III.iii.29-33)

Bardolph's nose is turned into a morality emblem, a symbol of sin and just punishment and an image of the hell-fire that awaits the recalcitrant transgressor. There is an accumulating humor in Falstaff's tongue-in-cheek moralizings in this play and in its sequel. But, for all the comic reverberations, his understanding of the death's head is clear and unequivocal. Its intention is contemplative; the observer learns from it and thinks about the consequences of actions. A reminder of earthly mortality, at the same time it stands as an exhortation to use the mortal condition as preparation for the day of judgment. Falstaff's comments, albeit comically, reach to the "official" significance of the death's head — a religious significance, a summoning to devotion. The sixteenth century memorial epigram to Thomas Gooding's "skeleton" (see *plate 19*) in Norwich Cathedral endorses this meaning:

> All you that do this place pass bye
> Remember death for you must dye.
> As you are now even so was I
> And as I am so shall you be.
> Thomas Gooding here do staye
> Wayting for God's judgement daye.

Yet, peculiarly, in the St. Alban's epitaph to John Hylocomius, the deceased is described as a "mere shade." In other words, a "mere" spirit who is no longer fleshed and alive. There is a rather odd indifference to church eschatology which offered a judgment of souls and an eternity of bliss to the righteous — but this peculiar harmony of religious message and secular regret is a not uncommon theme of Renaissance English funereal epitaphs and monuments.

* * * * *

In today's Denmark (read, England) it would be unthinkable to encounter a grave-digger who had casually tossed a skull next to the grave he was digging. But in the early modern period the sight would have been more common. Then, funerary practices frequently involved disinterment. A corpse, having been buried for a period in the grounds of a cemetery or, for the more affluent, under the flagstone in an adjoining church, was often disinterred. The bones, cleaned of whatever mortal debris still clung to them, were polished and piled in charnel houses. These were airy, arched wooden structures on the perimeters of churchyards in which the bones of the dead were neatly stacked and stored.[14] When Portia observes that she would "rather be married to a death's-head with a bone in his mouth" than to the Neopolitan Prince or the County Palentine, she perhaps has this sense of skeletal dismemberment in mind. Her inference is that the charnel process was a rather haphazard one. At its practical worst, this may indeed have been the case. The theory was considerably more organized, the idea being that skulls would be placed in one charnel room, leg bones in another, and so forth — everything in its rightful place — and that relatives, having paid for the service, should be able to visit their ancestors and offer due homage to their actual bones. None of the charnel houses of sixteenth century Europe survives today. They were highly susceptible to fire and the last great example, the vast Charnier et Cimetière des Innocents which contained the bones of more than a million souls, burnt down in the mid-seventeenth century.15 It was located adjacent to Paris' outdoor market, the Champeaux, a central and prominent feature of everyday life then as it remains today.

In the fifth act of *Hamlet*, the young hero of that play walks through the grounds of a graveyard, and chances across a skull — as John Jones puts it, "one of the most famous inanimate things in world drama."16 It is the skull of Yorick, one-time king's jester and young Hamlet's childhood idol. Harry Morris believes that the chief purpose of the graveyard scene is "to put Hamlet to a *memento-mori* experience."17 The episode acts, Morris suggests, as a reminder of the grave, bringing to Hamlet's attention the process of corruption to which all mortal bodies are inevitably subjected. Like Alexander and Caesar and Yorick, he will reach that point of desiccation in which he, too, is no more than a skull in a churchyard. What Hamlet must learn, Morris suggests, is that "rash and sinful action leads only to death" (p. 60). The problem with this argument, though, is that any kind of action will lead to death, be it rash, sinful or otherwise. I am led to doubt further Morris' claim by the evidence that he, Llewellyn, Frye, and many others, have provided as to the ubiquitous nature of *memento mori* in Renaissance Europe.18 This is hardly the first churchyard Hamlet has been in; and hardly the first death's head he has beheld. Why were the images and artifacts of the *memento mori* in the early modern age so profuse? Presumably because people did not trust themselves, or others, to learn or remember the lessons that the *memento mori* espoused. This, after all, is human nature. The more unpalatable or difficult rules of conduct need to be reiterated more frequently than those that are easier or more attractive to follow. Yet, the danger with reiterating necessities of action is that the urgency of the message can dissipate and even disappear over time. Sometimes an old message requires the shock of the new to restore its authority. Yorick's skull may be just that shock. What is different about this death's head is that Hamlet knows, or at least thinks he knows, to whom it belonged. It has therefore become "particularized" to the man who holds it in his hand and this, it seems to me, is what turns one of the most commonplace images of Shakespeare's day into the catalyst for a profound personal experience.

Michael Neill has suggested that "a cemetery is itself the most paradoxical of locations: at once a place of oblivion, and a site of memory; a place which annihilates all distinctions . . . and a site of monumental record; a place that both invites narrative and silences it."[19] Neill's point about cemeteries is a strong one but generalized. When we visit a graveyard there is, of course, a sense of annihilation that all of us share. As we survey the rows of crosses or flagstones or headstones or cairns our minds may well impose upon the funerary landscape that familiar template of mortal paradox: these stone signs represent lives that were and are no more, lives of foibles and dreams, triumphs and tragedies — and all now reduced to the silent uniformity of the grave. But when we visit graveyards, we also study gravestones. We particularize. We visit the graves of our relatives; we pause to reflect upon the epitaphs of those we never knew but whose lives were singularized by tragedy or longevity or oddity or some other distinguishing feature. I am saying "we" here when what I should be saying is "I," for this process is highly individualized. I share some deceased relatives with living others but aside from that there is no reason or expectation that the way I particularize the graves in a cemetery should duplicate the way someone else might do so.

Particularizing, for Hamlet, is not easy in the Elsinore graveyard. From what we know of Elizabethan churchyards, there were few inscripted flagstones or headstones, mostly only crosses to mark the graves. Records there were of people and their burial plots, but Hamlet leafing through the parish register would hardly have been a memorable stage spectacle. Shakespeare opts, instead, for a different means of allowing Hamlet to "particularize" — the living memory of a grave-digger who, having dug up a skull that has rested in the ground for seventeen years, is able fortuitously to identify it as that of Yorick, the old king's fool. The truth or a fanciful invention? It is just conceivable that the grave-diggers have come to that very spot on that very day precisely to dig up the bones of Yorick and to prepare a grave for Ophelia, those tasks accomplished efficiently in the same action. Yorick's bones would then be cleaned, polished and placed in the charnel house; and Ophelia's grave would be ready for her interment. Now, of course, there is a degree of fortuity in the fact that Hamlet is walking by at exactly *that* moment; but, as I have speculated already, it is not *entirely* stretching belief for the grave-digger to know whose skull he had unearthed. Whether correct or not, the information about Yorick's skull allows a name and identity to be attached. And Hamlet seems more than willing to believe the story.

I am moving a little ahead of myself here. Before Hamlet talks about the precise case of Yorick, he has more general observations to make about the skulls that are being thrown up from the grave.[20]

> *Hamlet.* That skull had a tongue in it, and could sing
> once. How the knave jowls it to the ground, as if
> 'twere Cain's jaw-bone, that did the first murder!
> This might be the pate of a politician, which this ass
> now o'erreaches, one that would circumvent God,
> might it not?
> *Horatio.* It might, my lord.
> *Hamlet.* Or of a courtier, which could say, "Good
> morrow, sweet lord! How dost thou, sweet lord?"
> This might be my Lord Such-a-one, that prais'd my
> Lord Such-a-one's horse when 'a meant to beg it, might it not?
> *Horatio.* Ay, my lord.

(V.i.75-87)

The particularization of mortality in this graveyard is very much Hamlet's particularization. Horatio's words stand largely as a laconic foil to the prince's commentary. The identities of the skulls are fashioned out of Hamlet's imagination. Perhaps this is the skull of a lawyer (lines 99-100)? Where, he asks a line later, are "his quiddities now, his quillities, his cases, his tenures, and his tricks?" And possibly this was a "great" buyer of land, with "his statutes, his recognizances, his fines, his double vouchers, his recoveries" (lines 104-6). The purchase and sale of land was, and still is, one of the most complex areas of English common and statutory law. Efforts were made in the first quarter of the twentieth century to simplify the processes involved, but with limited success. In Shakespeare's day, the prospective land purchaser had to be adroit in the intricacies of feudal land laws. Not only had he to be aware of the convoluted detail of prescription, easements, profits à prendre, adverse possession, fines — to name only a few — but he had also to have a command of language that could secure his documentation from the common prospect of judicial challenge. The assizes of King James I may have heard a few interesting witch trials but a greater bulk of their work centered on property disputes.

In each of the cases Hamlet nominates, we have examples of supreme intellectual and oratorical skill. His mode of particularization is built on his personal experiences and circumstances. All of these imagined illustrations of now-diminished mortality were, in their day, highly articulate and informed. The politician, that master of verbal duplicity, who "would circumvent God," has still perished. The courtier, expert in the subtleties of persuasion and innuendo, has not been able to flatter his way out of mortality's grip. The lawyer's dexterous quibbling and adroitness of argument have not beguiled Death. And the great land buyer, unparalleled in the infinite intricacies of conveyancing, now finds his genius encased in the grave, his "fine pate full of fine dirt" (lines 107-8). This passing parade of humankind is reminiscent of fourteenth century dance of death theatre, in which the twenty-four categories of social existence were each represented by an actor on stage, and then succumbed, one by one, to the summons of Death. Only *reminiscent* because Hamlet's social spectrum is somewhat narrower. He, of course, is an intellectual, an affluent university student from a court background, so it is not surprising that his conception of *memento mori* should focus on moneyed and upper class professionalism.

The universal message of *memento mori* is far wider than moneyed and upper class professionalism. It is, above all, a message about how Death, the leveler, "steals away the differences by and for which we live," to use Robert Watson's words.[21] It is on this point of "leveling" that Hamlet's understanding of the *memento mori* seems to fall short of the customary mark. In his imaginative particularization of skulls, he sees equality of mortal outcome within defined social parameters. His understanding of death is that it reduces great professional minds to nothingness. But the import of more standard representations of Death as the leveler — for example, Hans Holbein's dance of death series — is that leveling is a *social* leveling. In other words, great professional minds are reduced to the same kind of nothingness as the minds of peddlers. The point is captured succinctly in Simeoni's 1591 woodcut of a "a King's scepter, ioyned with a poore mans mattocke with a deaths heade betwixt them both" (see *plate 21*).[22] The death's head pointedly signifies the equalizing power of Death. The rich and the poor, the gifted and the untalented — all are leveled by the processes of mortal decay. This is the issue that eludes Hamlet. Curiously and significantly, even as he reminisces about the imagined professionalism of the skulls' owners, his descriptive asides referring to the grave-diggers figure precisely the lesson that he *should* be learning but which, for the moment, escapes his comprehension. He is irritated that the politician's skull is now jowled by a "knave" (line 76), that the courtier is now "knock'd about the mazzard with a sexton's spade" (lines 89-90), that a "mad knave" now hits the lawyer "about the sconce with a dirty shovel" (line 102), and that the skull of the great land buyer has been disturbed by clowns (lines 107-8). Before his very eyes, and apparently unrecognized, the delicacies and social gradations of mortal life are cast asunder, as working class sextons irreverently manhandle their erstwhile superiors and laugh while they are about it.

Intriguingly, the *memento mori* idea of social leveling is developed a step further in Hamlet's verbal duel with the grave-digger a few lines later in V.i. A working class man and yet a consummate master of language, the grave-digger gets the better of his aristocratic adversary in a wonderful exchange that echoes with all kinds of *memento mori* resonances. Whose grave is this, Hamlet demands of the grave-digger standing in the grave (lines 117-8)? Mine, sir, says the Clown. It may be, retorts Hamlet, since you are lying in it. And you, quips the Clown, are lying out of it. You lie, explains Hamlet, because you say its yours and, actually, it's a grave for the dead, not the living. Ah, smiles the Clown,

> 'Tis a quick lie, sir, 'twill away again from me to you.
> (lines 128-9)

In a sense, the grave-digger becomes a dance of death figure. Foolery was a common characteristic of Death in the *danse macabre*: in *Richard II*, he is called "antic" Death (III.ii.162); and in Marston's *The Malcontent* there is a comic interplay between Maria (hitherto supposed to be dead) and her husband Malevole, as he asks her dance:

> *Malevole.* Yes, more loved than our breath,
> With you I'll dance.
> *Maria.*   Why, then you dance with death.
> But come sir, I was ne'er more apt to mirth.
> (V.ii.108-9)[23]

For an instant, she takes on the witty rôle of Death in the *danse macabre* and, indeed, of the grave-digger in *Hamlet*, riposting the seriousness of her husband with frivolity and wordplay. Taunting and jesting with his victim-to-be, the Clown's mannerisms in *Hamlet* typify those of the antic

Death figure. Verbally dexterous, but with a darker meaning constantly
shadowing his wit, he toys remorselessly with his adversary. Hamlet,
distinctly uncomfortable, tries to withdraw from the duel and shifts the
subject. This is partly because he has been out-witted but also because
the Clown, in the tradition of the *memento mori*, has to have the last
word. This is YOUR grave, Hamlet. It is yours because the living
become the dead, be they prince or pauper. The young royal has himself
been metaphorically battered about the head by this low caste "knave"
(line 137) who, with somewhat heavy irony, remains standing in the
grave as he does so. Has Hamlet at last understood the lesson? His
effort to slide out of the debate with the Clown undoubtedly signals
discomfort, but his lack of candor in defeat suggests also a man still
caught somewhere between denial and illumination.

Robert Watson, referring to the first act of the play where Hamlet
immediately repeats his mother's assertion that death is "common"
(I.ii.72), has argued that it is "precisely the commonness of death that
horrifies him, the way it erases distinctions."[24] In the grave-diggers'
scene, though, it is not the commonness of death that horrifies Hamlet
for he is perfectly able to "distinguish" between the skulls imaginatively
(this a courtier, this a lawyer, and so forth), and even in affirming that a
diminution has occurred he seems less than horror-struck. By contrast,
he is filled with repulsion by the *smell* of Yorick's skull — a skull to
which he is able to attach memory and, therefore, distinction.

> *1 Clown.*   This same
> skull, sir, was, sir, Yorick's skull, the King's jester.
> *Hamlet.* This?   [*Takes the skull.*]
> *1 Clown.* E'en that.
> *Hamlet.* Alas poor Yorick! I knew him, Horatio, a
> fellow of infinite jest, of most excellent fancy. He
> hath bore me on his back a thousand times, and now
> how abhorr'd in my imagination it is! my gorge rises
> at it. Here hung those lips that I have kiss'd I know not
> how oft. Where be your gibes now, your gambols,
> your songs, your flashes of merriment, that were
> wont to set the table on a roar? Not one now to mock
> your own grinning — quite chop-fall'n? Now get you
> to my lady's chamber, and tell her, let her paint an

inch thick, to this favor she must come; make her
laugh at that. Prithee, Horatio, tell me one thing.
   Horatio. What's that, my lord?
   Hamlet. Dost thou think Alexander look'd a' this
fashion i' th' earth?
   Horatio. E'en so.
   Hamlet. And smelt so? pah!   [*Puts down the skull.*]
   Horatio. E'en so, my lord.
   Hamlet. To what base uses we may return, Horatio!
Why may not imagination trace the noble dust of
Alexander, till 'a find it stopping a bunghole?
   Horatio. E'en so.

(V.i.180-205)

Hamlet, whose thoughts had been locked within a narrow social range of
mortal reduction, now acknowledges the full social spectrum of the
memento mori. Many commentators have noticed the allusion to what
they presume to be the dance of death in Hamlet's suggestion that the
"grinning" skull should be sent "to my lady's chamber, and tell her, let
her paint an inch thick, to this favor she must come." Strictly speaking,
it is not an allusion to the *danse macabre* but to the death's head which is
often represented with a grinning demeanor. That aside, Hamlet's words
are certainly an expression of universal mortality but they go a step
beyond that. They are, as importantly, an affirmation of death's function
as social equalizer. However much make-up Queen Gertrude applies to
her face, she will still be reduced to the same state as the jester Yorick.
In the lines that follow, the mortal fate of the fool Yorick is also paralleled
to that of the emperor Alexander — from the ridiculous to the sublime,
the end of physical life reduces *all* mortal beings to the same dusty
denominator. As Hamlet asks Horatio a series of questions, the answers
to which he already knows, his companion's "E'en so" tolls with somber
certitude.

    There is an interesting comparison to be made between Hamlet's
response to Yorick's skull and Vendice's response to his murdered
mistress' skull, which he carries round with him for much of the action
of *The Revenger's Tragedy.* Tourneur's hero addresses Gloriana's skull
early in the first scene of the play:

Thou sallow picture of my poisoned love,
                    [*Views the skull in his hand.*]
My study's ornament, thou shell of death,
Once the bright face of my betrothed lady,
When life and beauty naturally filled out
These ragged imperfections. . . .
                    (I.i.14-18)[25]

For him, the skull is a *memento* of the injustice committed against his
mistress, and the focal point and stimulus for his drive towards revenge.
Even more than this, it becomes a metaphor for the inexorable processes
of retribution, symbolizing not simply the idea that death comes to
everyone but, more particularly, that this specific crime cannot be washed
away and forgotten and that its memory recurs as certainly as death
itself. In this last sense, Vendice's death's head has more in common
with Banquo's ghost or *Hamlet*'s "play within a play" than it does with
Yorick's skull. Unlike Hamlet, Vendice is not simply content to converse
with and about Gloriana's skull (as he does often enough), but he moves
further to emblematize it into theatrical action. So, he engages, at one
point (III.iv.90 et seq.), in a bizarre mime in which he feeds a cup of
poison to the skull, mirroring the mortal crime that took Gloriana's life
in the first place. Then, later in the same scene, he executes an elaborate
stage spectacle in which he poisons her murderer (the Duke) and lights
up the skull with a torch so that the Duke in his last moments of life is
forced to gaze with terror into the fiery, animated eyes of Death (III.iv.130-
1).

I suspect that our modern sensibilities have tutored us to respond to
images of the skull with greater revulsion than was the normative case in
Shakespeare's time. *The Revenger's Tragedy* dramatizes the death's head
to unusual extremity. Though *Hamlet* is a play about revenge, the death's
head does not serve the ends of terror that it does in Tourneur's work.
For a start, Shakespeare presents the object to us in a less threatening
circumstance; and, initially at least, allows his young hero to respond to
the image intellectually rather than emotionally. Yorick's skull does not
spur Hamlet to a spasm of revengeful invective or melancholic dejection;
for the most part, it encourages him to quiet and measured reflection.
The point is well made by Frye who has suggested that "If we view the
graveyard scene in Elsinore only or even primarily in terms of those
typically twentieth-century attitudes which seek to ignore or euphemize

death, we may regard Hamlet at this point as morbid in soul and sick in mind. But if we reestablish the sixteenth-century context . . . we see a Hamlet here thinking through the ultimate realities of death to arrive at what becomes, for him as it had for others, a new sanity and even serenity."26 This view holds good up to the point where Hamlet casts down the skull. But then a brutal reality impinges on the intellectual drive towards sanity and serenity. Until Hamlet balks at Yorick's skull ("Pah!") and throws it to the ground, there has been no hint of stark confrontation with the full actuality of death comparable to that so powerfully, even histrionically, emblematized in *The Revenger's Tragedy*. On the contrary, until its final moments the action of *Hamlet* seems almost deliberately to foster the sanitization and intellectualization of death.27 Claudius killed Hamlet's father, true, but young Hamlet never saw it — the ghost recounts the crime. Yes, Hamlet slays Polonius but it doesn't quite happen in open view. Polonius is stabbed through the arras (III.iv.24), a heavy tapestry that closed off a small room at the back of the stage. Hamlet draws back the arras to see the body. Not even he, in this sanitized version of mortality, witnesses the murder he has committed. Rosencrantz and Guildenstern are dispatched to their deaths by a document that Hamlet has cunningly altered, but neither we, nor Hamlet, will witness the spectacle of their beheading. Ophelia, perhaps driven to insanity by Hamlet's mystifying behavior, takes her own life. In fact, as he holds Yorick's skull, Hamlet does not even know that she is dead and that the arrival of her funeral cortège is imminent.

These I call "santizations" of death in the play because they sanitize fatality by placing an experiential layer between the detail of death and Hamlet's knowledge of it. At no point before the final scene of the play does he get blood on his hands; at no point until then does he see the face of a victim at the actual moment of death. In our own age, we can well understand this kind of sanitization. I am haunted by Glenn McNatt's description of an official Khmer Rouge photograph, taken in the charnel house years of modern Cambodia:

> She is a girl of about 12, and she faces the camera with the calm composure of an innocent. Behind her is a blank wall or perhaps a sheet tacked up as a makeshift backdrop. Nothing in the picture suggests that the child is an enemy of the state, or that she will shortly be executed for her crimes. . . . To gaze on the face of a 12-year-old victim is to be struck dumb by the horror that lies just outside the picture frame. The mind comprehends this child is no more, but heart

and eye rebel at the notion. In vain one searches that open countenance for evidence of high treason. "What did you do, little girl, to deserve torture and death?" And her eyes reply: "I did nothing. I am innocent."[28]

Of course, we feel pain when we read this or see the photograph but the true savagery of the girl's death is outside the picture or the words, it is beyond our experience. We understand what has happened, we have knowledge of it, but unless we were there and put the plastic bag over her head or felt the bag being put over ours, there is still an experiential arras between the girl's death and our response to it.

In such situations, a natural inclination is to intellectualize. From our sanitized position, we seek to articulate the dimensions and the nature and the motivations of suffering. Hamlet, as one perpetually shielded from harsh reality, responds exactly in this way. From his intellectual vantage point, he speculates beautifully about the owners of the skulls: the lawyer, the politician, the great land owner, the courtier. But when, with certainty, he holds in his hands the skull, the *actual* skull, of Yorick, the skull whose lips he had once kissed, whose cheeks he had pinched, the reality is overwhelming:

> *Hamlet.* Dost thou think Alexander look'd a' this
> fashion i' th' earth?
> *Horatio.* E'en so.
> *Hamlet.* And smelt so? pah! [*Puts down the skull.*]

Hamlet's intellectualizing at last fails him. He tries vainly to rationalize Yorick's skull, to draw an erudite and touching parallel, but the sanitizing veneer is no longer there. The flesh of his hand touches the bone of the skull; the stench of rotten death fills his nostrils. "Pah!" he balks, and flings down the skull of the man he loved. The response is derived from Hamlet's physical disgust but perhaps compounded by what R. A. Foakes has identified as "a deep anxiety that there may be nothing beyond the grave."[29] This play is replete with speculation about the ramifications of this act or that, about conduct appropriate for salvation and actions determining damnation. There is, I think, an interesting process of contrasting taking place between intellectual responses to mortality and the gross reality of death.[30] The death's head is an important discursive figure in this process; but so, too, are issues of heaven and hell which recur profusely in the language of the play.

You might have supposed, given Hamlet's propensity for other-world allusion (angel, devil, purgatory, and so forth), that his thoughts in the final moments of life would have moved in that direction. Not so. As life slips from him in Act V, his emphasis is on the mortal world. There can be no longer a certitude of progression to heaven or hell or anything beyond the grave. Instead, his words revert to the idea of Death as a physical entity rather than as a vehicle for further spiritual travel:

> You that look pale and tremble at this chance,
> That are but mutes or audience to this act,
> Had I but time — as this fell sergeant, Death,
> Is strict in his arrest — O, I could tell you —
> But let it be.
>
> (V.ii.334-8)[31]

The "sergeant, Death," as Harry Morris has demonstrated, is a clear reference to a specific type of dance of death tableau.[32] Those pale and trembling people he addresses, the "mutes or audience to this act," are the same persons intellectually removed from the actuality of his death. They have witnessed what has happened, but they have not killed or been killed. There is an experiential arras between them and the events they have seen. Hamlet's realization seems to be, as the fell sergeant Death approaches him like the grinning dance of death figure in Martinelli's painting, that there can be no full bridging of the gulf between intellectualized death and actual death. Those who have not looked into the hollow eyes of Death simply cannot understand it wholly, cannot know its fullest truths. "O, I could tell you —" he begins but then changes his mind. "But let it be."

That Hamlet is able to talk with resigned coherence in his last moments, rather than succumbing with mute terror to the advance of Death, is some evidence that mortality may be less frightening than Yorick's skull had suggested. Perhaps, after all, the rituals of verbalization and contemplation have helped Hamlet come to terms better with the ephemeral qualities of life. A woodcut print, facing the title page of John Daye's edition of Hugh Latimer's *Seven Sermons made vpon the Lordes Prayer* (London, 1571), may be instructive here. It shows two men discussing a skeleton out of whose stomach cavity grows a tree. Talking about death, even academicizing it, as a means of comprehending and fearing it less, has a history perhaps as long as humanity itself.

Latimer's sermons, delivered and published long before Shakespeare came to the stage, are, of course, founded on religious certainties. It is for the individual to make his intellectual peace with the idea of death, projecting himself into the future and confronting the specter of mortality. Patricia Carlin makes the interesting point that "The construction of *Hamlet* imitates entrapment within a single, death-tainted body. We see almost always through Hamlet's eyes; for part of what the play is depicting is what is entailed in existence within an irreducibly individual self: isolation; limit (of knowledge, or efficacy); death."[33] Hamlet's exploration of his mortality, his awareness of death as the "undiscover'd country" (III.i.78) and his willingness to image his own physical demise through "projective memory,"[34] as Engel terms it, sustains him in the final moments of his life. His intellectualizations, perhaps tentative and sentimentalized and even deficient at first, somehow find a kind of vindication in the dignity and coherence of his own passing.

Notes

1. Giovanni Martinelli (1610-1659) was a Florentine influenced by the innovations of Caravaggio. The painting is housed in the New Orleans Museum of Art.
2. William E. Engel, *Mapping Mortality: The Persistence of Memory and Melancholy in Early Modern England* (Amherst: University of Massachusetts Press, 1995), p. 67.
3. The marble cadavers at Salisbury Cathedral, Wiltshire, stand atop the tombs of Thomas Bennett (Precentor and Acting Dean 1542-1558) and George Sydenham (Archdeacon of Sarum 1503-1524, and Chaplain to King Henry VII and King Henry VIII).
4. Thomas Kyd's *The Spanish Tragedy*, ed. J. R. Mulryne, in *Elizabethan and Jacobean Tragedies: A New Mermaid Anthology*, introduced by Brian Gibbons (Tonbridge, Kent: Ernest Benn, 1984).
5. Roland Mushat Frye, *The Renaissance Hamlet: Issues and Responses in 1600* (Princeton: Princeton University Press, 1984), p. 207.
6. Nigel Llewellyn, *The Art of Death: Visual Culture in the English Death Ritual c. 1500 - c. 1800* (London: Reaktion Books, in association with the Victoria and Albert Museum, 1991), p. 26.
7. Frye, pp. 210-11.
8. A seventeenth century monument to the Nicholas family adjacent to the front portal inside Gloucester Cathedral includes a death's head and hourglass. Similarly, the 1601 death monument to Anne Markham immediately to the right of the entrance to the Parish Church of St. Mary Magdalene at Newark-on-Trent in Nottinghamshire (*plate 2*) reveals an hourglass and skull.
9. The original mechanisms of the clock have been long lost. The clock face and movement were made in Plymouth in the early years of the nineteenth century. The organ is thought to be German, from around about the same time. When the organ is set in motion, the skeletons ring the bells above them. Spanish prisoners of war, at first housed in the Spanish Barn at Torquay and subsequently imprisoned at nearby Dartmoor Jail, carved the clock's casing. Many of the figures reflect Iberian fashions of the time, but the death's head warning at the top of the clock was a symbol every sixteenth century European would have understood.
10. Claude Paradin, *The Heroicall Devises* (London: 1591), p. 319 (motto: "Victory is the end"), represents a death's head crowned with a laurel garland. Paradin's commentary is a celebration of death, describing how the Emperor Adrianus explained that the heads of the dead were crowned with garlands to show "that by death they had ouercome the labors, sorrows and imminent heape of the cares of this life" (p. 319).

11. Simeoni's *Pvrtratvres Or Emblemes of Gabriel Simeon, a Florentine* (London: 1591), p. 373 (wrongly numbered 273 in the 1591 printing), appends the following commentary to a picture of a death's head which surmounts a crossed scepter and hoe: "Princes, noble men, rich men, and finallie all men of what authoritie or condition so euer they be, ought diligently to looke into this picture of a Kings scepter, ioyned with a poore mans mattocke with a deaths heade betwixt them both, with these wordes: *Mors sceptra ligonibus aequans*, Death maketh Kings scepters equall to pore mens mattocks."

12. Geffrey Whitney, *A Choice of Emblemes* (Leyden: Christopher Plantin, 1586), p. 229.

13. Cyril Tourneur, *The Atheist's Tragedy* in *John Webster and Cyril Tourneur: Four Plays*, ed. John Addington Symonds (New York: Hill and Wang, 1966).

14. The practice of locating the body parts of a deceased person in different places had been well established since early Medieval times. For example, on the death of King John II of France in 1364, sometime prisoner of Edward the Black Prince, the monarch's heart was sent to Canterbury for burial. For a discussion of charnel houses, see Philippe Ariès, *Western Attitudes toward Death: From the Middle Ages to the Present*, trans. Patricia M. Ranum (Baltimore: The Johns Hopkins University Press, 1974), pp. 18-23.

15. There is only one known print of the Charnier et Cimetière des Innocents, Paris — a sixteenth century Flemish depiction in the Musée Carnavalet, Paris. The practice of bone decoration in Europe ended only in the eighteenth century, and examples remain extant in Rome at the Capuchin Church and in the small church behind the Farnese Palace, where bones have been used to construct various ornaments. See Ariès, pp. 20-2.

16. John Jones, *Shakespeare at Work* (Oxford: The Clarendon Press, 1995), p. 71. Jones' study of the folio and quarto versions of the scene is wittily and incisively presented in the same work, especially pp. 71-9. For a perceptive account of the layers of meaning in the scene, see Martin W. Walsh, "'This same skull, Sir . . .': Layers of Meaning and Tradition in Shakespeare's most famous Prop," *Hamlet Studies: An International Journal of Research on the Tragedie of Hamlet, Prince of Denmarke* (New Delhi, India), 9 (1987), pp. 65-77. Frye, p. 206, notes that, as far as modern scholarship can determine, Shakespeare's use of the graveyard scene was "a striking innovation on the London stage."

17. Harry Morris, *Last Things in Shakespeare* (Tallahassee: Florida State University Press, 1985), p. 60.

18. Llewellyn, for example, records that "Death 'himself' is the main actor in the countless variants of the *memento mori* imagery which survive: he scythes through the ranks of the proud, creeps up on the unwary with his

bow and plague arrow, frightens all and sundry. His lack of respect for social degree and his indiscriminate behaviour were especially terrifying. He grins, allows near escapes, he always conquers. His expressionless features deny the powerful inherent semiotic quality of the human face, and signify a separate kind of existence, 'the other' to the living human. This skull appears on even modest domestic paraphernalia, including spoons . . . and snuff-boxes . . . , as well as in didactic arts, such as in woodcuts, illustrations in books or, like the *Judd Marriage*, as separate pictures designed to hang on the wall. In early modern England Death always accompanied the individual on the streets or at home among the family" (p. 26).

19. Michael Neill, *Issues of Death: Mortality and Identity in English Renaissance Tragedy* (Oxford: Clarendon Press, 1997), p. 234.
20. Robert N. Watson, *The Rest is Silence: Death as Annihilation in the English Renaissance* (Berkeley: University of California Press, 1994), p. 89, has suggested that the grave-digging scene is a parody of the Last Judgement, in which "skulls rise from their graves to endure Hamlet's sentences." If so, the only resurrection it can provide, as Watson (p. 89) concedes, is that of exhumation.
21. Watson, p. 98.
22. Simeoni, p. 373. See also Guillaume de la Perrière, *La Morosophie de Guillaume de la Perriere Tolosain, Contenant Cent Emblemes moraux* (Lyon: Bonhomme, 1553), emblem 99, where a skeletal Death weighs the accoutrements of kingship against the agrarian implements of a poor man. And the scales rest absolutely level.
23. John Marston, *The Malcontent and Other Plays*, ed. Keith Sturgess (Oxford: Oxford University Press, 1997).
24. Watson, p. 80.
25. Cyril Tourneur, *The Revenger's Tragedy* in *John Webster and Cyril Tourneur: Four Plays*, ed. John Addington Symonds (New York: Hill and Wang, 1966).
26. Frye, p. 220.
27. For a valuable discussion of the frenetic overlapping of ideas in *Hamlet*, relevant perhaps to the sense of intellectualization I have argued for here, see Philip Davis, *Sudden Shakespeare: The Shaping of Shakespeare's Creative Thought* (London: Athlone, 1996), pp. 84-7.
28. Glenn McNatt's column in *The Baltimore Sun* (Internet edition at www.sunspot.net/columnists/data/mcnatt/072797mcnatt.html), 27 July 1997, titled "Cambodians stare at us, and ask why they must die," referred to a photograph in an exhibition titled "The Killing Fields" which ran through the summer of 1997 at the Museum of Modern Art in New York.
29. R. A. Foakes, *Hamlet Versus Lear: Cultural Politics and Shakespeare's Art* (Cambridge: Cambridge University Press, 1993), p. 173. See, also,

Michael Neill, "'Exeunt with a Dead March': Funeral Pageantry on the Shakespearean Stage," *Pageantry in the Shakespearean Theater*, ed. David M. Bergeron (Athens: University of Georgia Press, 1985) pp. 153-93.

30. Undoubtedly, this dissonance between experience and non-experience works itself out on a theatrical level too — between the actor who pretends and the actor who feels. Hamlet's advice to the players on the art of acting speaks exactly to this issue, as Pauline Kiernan has shown in her book *Shakespeare's Theory of Drama* (Cambridge: Cambridge University Press, 1996), pp. 125-6.

31. The dance of death maintains a muted but certain presence in *Hamlet*. Frye sees the poetic *danse macabre* imaged in references to two of its memorable figures: when Hamlet thinks of Yorick's skull he recalls the idea of the jester; and when he considers sending the skull to "my lady" as an illustration of the futility of cosmetics, his lady could be any one of the many handsome female figures carried off in images of the dance of death (pp. 238-9).

32. Harry Morris, "The Dance of Death in Shakespeare," *Papers on Language and Literature*, 20 (1984), p. 27: "The Sergeant is a figure found in almost all the traditional Dances as a type seized by the skeleton. He appears at Holy Innocents and at St. Paul's; if Stow's reference to the paintings at the guildhall in Stratford as the 'Daunce of Powles' means that the two were identical, then the Sergeant was present in Warwickshire as well. Furthermore, the Sergeant marches in Lydgate's Daunce of Machabree where he responds to his summons with these words: 'Howe durste thou Death set on me arest'. . . . The combination of the sergeant figure, the word *arrest*, and the inability to flee (or strictness of the arrest) suggests that Lydgate might be Shakespeare's source for the image in *Hamlet*."

33. Patricia L. Carlin, *Shakespeare's Mortal Men: Overcoming Death in History, Comedy and Tragedy* (New York: Peter Lang, 1993), p. 222.

34. Engel, p. 68.

Chapter 6

ℰℭℛ

Experiments with the Danse Macabre

The dance of death was originally a species of theatre that developed in fourteenth century Germany and France but acquired rapid popularity throughout Europe in the fifteenth century.[1] Plays were usually held in the grounds of a cemetery, with some of the action emanating from adjoining charnel houses. The drama would begin with a sermon from a religious personage in which members of the audience were exhorted to remember the imminence of death and to prepare themselves accordingly. In due course two or more Death figures would emerge from a neighboring charnel house. In order to convey the appropriate fear of the moment, the actors playing Death would be wearing a close fitting suit made from linen, upon which the skeletal structure of the human body had been outlined in yellow paint. The impression given was of moving, living skeletons. Advancing forth to an assembled host of actors, microcosmically representing the world's society, one specter would approach a member of that society and announce that the moment of death had arrived. The victim, often represented as a king or cardinal, would politely decline the invitation, pleading some prior engagement or obligation. But Death could not be assuaged and when the arguments ran out, the crest-fallen victim would be led away. In due course, the other Death figures would advance to claim their prey: soldiers, popes, emperors, peddlers — the full spectra of mortal life. It became customary for these macabre messengers to perform a little jig as they entered and left the stage, perhaps in grim imitation of the cosmic dance which held all things, living and dead, in universal harmony. The play would end with another sermon, affirming that Death was the great leveler and that none could escape his skeletal grasp. This is fundamentally the message of the play *Everyman*, an evolved species of the *danse macabre*, though here text and, probably, performance had become more subtle and professionalized.[2]

The Death figure of the early plays was intended as a frightening persona but iconographic representations of him on church walls, in books, and all manner of artifacts from pottery to muskets, drew him to new heights of popularity in the fifteenth and sixteenth centuries. Iconographically, the celebrated 1425 mural in the Charnier et Cimetière des Innocents, Paris, was probably the oldest, and certainly the most imitated, *danse macabre* series.[3] Though demolished in the seventeenth century, the detail of the series was preserved in a 1485 French manuscript.[4] The Englishman, John Lydgate, visited the Innocents in Paris, also copying its images and translating its written commentaries. In turn, his work is known to have inspired *danse macabre* representations in various English church and cathedral settings: a series of paintings in the cloister of Pardon Churchyard, near St. Paul's Cathedral; a mural at Hexham Priory in Northumberland; another at the Parish Church of St. Mary Magdalene at Newark-on-Trent; a sculpted column at Boxgrove Priory near Chichester; and wood carvings in the misereres of the Drapers' Chapel at Coventry Cathedral in the West Midlands. The Pardon cloister was demolished in 1549; and the wood carvings at Coventry completely destroyed in a bombing raid in 1940.[5] Only remnants remain at Hexham Priory and St. Mary Magdalene at Newark-on-Trent (*plate 17*). The solitary dance of death figure reaching for the hand of a reticent maiden in the de la Warr Chapel at Boxgrove Priory is almost fully intact (*plate 20*). To these we may add the sixteenth century skeleton at Norwich Cathedral who, though not strictly in the tradition, nonetheless captures its spirit with his smirking grin and his bony hands clasped mockingly in prayer (*plate 19*). An impressive *danse macabre* series may also have existed in the Grove Chapel, at Stratford-on-Avon and, if so, Shakespeare would likely have been familiar with it.[6] On the European continent, *danse macabre* motifs have survived in better condition. Startling depictions may be seen in the frescoes in the Chapel of Kernascléden in Brittany; and in the remarkable sixty foot long mural at the Church of St. Mary in Berlin, prompted by the plague of 1484. One of the most haunting and vivid presentations is to be found in a late Medieval fresco in the Church of St. Mary at Beram (Istria) in Croatia, revealing the representatives of society, adults and children, being led to the grave by an assortment of jigging, grinning, scythe-bearing and trumpeting skeletal figures. The trumpet was one of the most familiar motifs of the *danse macabre*, and was popular, too, in theatrical descriptions of death, as in *Everyman* where the unfortunate hero, reflecting on his false friends, sadly realizes that "whan Deth bloweth his blast, / They all renne fro me full fast" (lines 843-4).[7]

In book iconography, skeletal Death is evoked with equal consternation. A woodcut by Michael Wolgemut in Hartman Schedel's *Liber Chronicum* (1493) records the awakening of the emissaries of death.[8] Four figures, summoned from rest, perform a little jig while a fifth of their party disentangles himself from his shroud and prepares to arise from the grave. In other texts, as in the early sixteenth century *Danse Macabre* from Troyes, Death figures, grinning and taunting and occasionally bearing scythes, lead off their victims in a grotesque illustration of the invincibility of Death.[9] A prancing irresistible fiend, the dance of death figure stalks the mortal world with a rather smug grin on his bony face. Very occasionally in plays of the period, as in *The Knight of the Burning Pestle*, Death is caricatured as a kind of scallywag — inventively trying to drum up business by mischievously slipping into a shop, wearing a tradesman's blue apron, in order "To cheapen *Aqua-vitae*" (V.iii.155)[10] and then, having been discovered two lines later, throwing pepper in people's eyes to make good his escape. Such usage is highly unusual, though. Death, in the theatre and iconography of Shakespeare's age, is routinely a force of considerable fear; and a fear perhaps exacerbated by the processes of burial and charnel housing in the great cemeteries of sixteenth century Europe. Human nature being what it is, we can rest assured that people imagined all these bones somehow reassembled themselves and danced and musicked through the night until the first rays of dawn drove them back to rest in the charnel houses. This idea is suggested in the work of Hans Holbein the Younger in the first half of the sixteenth century, perhaps the most celebrated iconographic representations of the dance of death ever created on page, canvas or wall.

In the fifth print of Holbein's *Imagines Mortis* (1545), titled "Bones of All Men," a band of living skeletons enjoy themselves outside a charnel house, banging drums and blowing trumpets and generally having a good time.[31] Around their feet there are assorted body parts, suggesting that the process of reassemblage (as ever is the case) threw up items surplus to requirements. There are more than fifty prints in Holbein's dance of death series, published between 1538 and 1562, most of them depicting skeleton Death figures mingling in the mortal world.[12] Sometimes these gangly fiends act as disinterested and unobserved spectators, rather like Spenser's "dreadfull Death [who] behind thy backe doth stond" (*The Faerie Queene*, II.viii.37)[13]; but mostly they are portrayed in full flight, advancing upon or seizing a victim. "The Abbot" (print xiv) is a brilliant illustration of the power and arrogance of Death. Having selected his victim, skeleton Death tugs him away by the gown. In a sign of utter irreverence, Death has donned the cleric's miter and has slung his crosier over his shoulder — an unsavory mimicry that William Engel has noticed in a variety of *danse macabre* representations.[14] He grins inanely as he marches off. The abbot resists, of course, his right hand trying to thrust off his attacker. All to no avail. The moment has come for the great leveler to claim him, a fact affirmed by the hourglass that sits almost unnoticed on the branch of a nearby tree.

Holbein's work was enormously popular in England, and he was renowned across Europe for two masterly studies of the dance of death.[15] The first, *Les Simulachres & Historiees faces de la Mort*, was published in Lyon in 1538, and the production of a third edition (newly titled *Imagines Mortis*) in Latin by 1542 confirmed its cross-European importance.[16] After the first edition in 1538, ten further (and progressively enlarged) editions followed over the next twenty-four years. The book was extensively pirated, with five such editions appearing in Cologne, for example, in the twenty years from 1555.[17] It was also the subject of prolific and inferior imitation, with probably more than a hundred versions appearing in the sixteenth century alone.[18] The second, *Icones Historiarvm Veteris Testamenti* (1547), though not quite as popular, was nonetheless translated into English within two years and produced in numerous other vernaculars across Europe in the decades that followed.[19]

It is most probable that Shakespeare was familiar with both works. Certainly, his theatre makes explicit reference to the idea of death as a living thing, usually the "lean and abhorred monster" of *Romeo and Juliet* (V.iii.102-5) but not always so:

                    for within the hollow crown
            That rounds the mortal temples of a king
            Keeps Death his court, and there the antic sits,
            Scoffing his state and grinning at his pomp. . . .
                            (Richard, *Richard II* III.ii.160-3)

            Death, death; O amiable lovely death!
            Thou odoriferous stench! sound rottenness!
            Arise forth from the couch of lasting night,
            Thou hate and terror to prosperity,
            And I will kiss thy detestable bones. . . .
                            (Lady Constance, *King John* III.iv.25-9)

            Menenius.   every gash was an
            enemy's grave. [*A shout and flourish.*] Hark, the
            trumpets.
                Volumnia. These are the ushers of Marcius: before him
            he carries noise, and behind him he leaves tears:
            Death, that dark spirit, in 's nervy arm doth lie,
            Which, being advanc'd, declines, and then men die.
                    A sennet. Trumpets sound.
                            (*Coriolanus* II.i.155-61)

Death as the scoffer of pomp; Death as an amiable attendant; Death as an
insuperable warrior. The significances, as we shall see, can shift not
only between plays but within them as well. So, too, the emotional
constructions alter. The Death of *Romeo and Juliet* is a repulsive monster,
a source of revulsion and rejection; but that of *King John*, though
"detestable," is still "amiable" and desired. Equally, Coriolanus' Death-
like qualities distinguish him from the common run of men, and valorize
him as such; but the Death of *Richard II* serves to remind all and sundry
that he is the great leveler, a force that reduces all living things, however
grand or elevated their mortal station.[20]

    It is my purpose in the pages that follow to explore three variations
of the dance of death *topos* — Death as the leveler; Death as the benign
guardian; and Death as a metaphor for superlative soldiership.

                        * * * * *

The sense of earthly transience lies at the heart of the dance of death dialectic. The temporary nature of mortality, topically accentuated by intermittent plague outbreaks in the latter part of the sixteenth century, was embedded in the Elizabethan psyche. Not surprisingly, such views were regularly rehearsed in religious contexts, as in Andrew Willet's *Sacrorum Emblematum Centuria Una* ("we are all of earthly traine, and must away")[21] or in this sixteenth century memorial poem to Amie Wiatt on a brass plaque in the nave of Tewkesbury Abbey:

> A me disce mores est sors omnibus una;
> Mortis et esca fui, mortis et esca fores

> (Learn from me at my death that all are doomed to die:
> My life was food for death; in turn, you will become as I.)

Sentiments like these were commonly expressed, as well, in secular emblematizations where there is often a codicillary reminder that, whatever the achievements of mortal endeavor, "The Prince, the poore, are laid in graues alike."[22]

Shakespearean characters are occasionally apt to reflect upon this truism. For example, his kingdom collapsing around him, King Richard has cause in *Richard II* to ponder the state of monarchical mortality. The speculations reverberate darkly. The word "hollow" is connected with falsehood as early as I.iv.9 when Aumerle describes to the king his "hollow parting" with Hereford. It gathers a foreboding momentum through its association with the "hollow eyes of death" at II.i.270, and with the grave at III.ii.140, and may be related to the notion of the hollow womb in the fallen English paradise. By the time it serves Richard's antic Death allusion, it has been well established as a key term in the nomenclature of what I described in an earlier chapter as a fallen English Eden.

> within the hollow crown
> That rounds the mortal temples of a king
> Keeps Death his court, and there the antic sits,
> Scoffing his state and grinning at his pomp,
> Allowing him a breath, a little scene,
> To monarchize, be fear'd, and kill with looks,
> Infusing him with self and vain conceit,

As if this flesh which walls about our life
Were brass impregnable; and, humor'd thus,
Comes at the last and with a little pin
Bores through his castle wall, and farewell king!
                                         (III.ii.160-70)

Douce (1807) was the first to suggest that the seventh print in Holbein's *Imagines Mortis*, "The Emperor," may have inspired these lines.[23]   In this print the emperor is holding court and dispensing justice, sword in hand (*plate 22*). To his right, a courtier seems to be the subject of ire; and, on his left, a poor supplicant kneels in dutiful obedience. The omnipresent hourglass sits at his feet, its sands of time fast running out. Behind the emperor, unnoticed and engrossed, a smiling skeletal Death grasps the emperor's crown with his left hand and with his right reaches inside the hollow round of the crown, perhaps even into the emperor's skull. It could just be, and some have speculated this is so,[24] that the skeletal Death merely grasps the other side of the crown with his right hand — and that the cut simply fails slightly on an artistic level to reproduce that effect. This seems unlikely. Holbein's command of artistic design was unsurpassed, and the technical accomplishment of his engraver, Lützelburger, set a benchmark standard for the century that followed. Also, Death's left hand does not appear to be grasping the crown but resting upon it supportively — as, indeed, we would expect were the other hand reaching inside to grasp or pull out something. The skeleton's left leg is at right angles to the body, again suggesting the leverage necessary for delving into the crown rather than just lifting it off. Harry Morris, in summation, has suggested that, to his scrutiny, "hardly a word in Richard's self-portrait lacks a parallel to the woodcut."[25]

   If Shakespeare was influenced by the print, then his text took matters even further, suggesting that Death was actually sitting within the "hollow crown / That rounds the mortal temples of a king." This is "Scoffing" and "grinning" Death at his most frightening. He is Death the clown, but the joke is on his victims.[26] Within this narrow mortal sphere, the emperor may be all-powerful, instilling fear and dread into his subjects through even a glance. But he is only mortal, and no more impregnable to the onslaught of Death than those his subjects over whom he monarchizes. The idea of Death as the siegeman ("and with a little pin / Bores through his castle wall") is in the vein of familiar military images that Shakespeare attaches to the idea of antic Death in the other English history plays (for example, *King John* at V.vii.15-20; and *Henry V* at IV.ii.39-42). Elsewhere in *Richard II*, the dance of death figures powerfully:

> My inch of taper will be burnt and done,
> And blindfold death not let me see my son.
> (I.iii.223-4)

> I will despair, and be at enmity
> With cozening hope. He is a flatterer,
> A parasite, a keeper-back of death,
> Who gently would dissolve the bands of life,
> Which false hope lingers in extremity.
> (II.ii.68-72)

> Cry woe, destruction, ruin, and decay:
> The worst is death, and death will have his day. . . .
> (III.ii.102-3)

> How now, what means death in this rude assault?
> (V.v.105)

These images of the *danse macabre* vary considerably. The idea of life as a candle ("my inch of taper") is familiar in the emblem books and often associated with the death's head — as, for example, in George Wither's twenty-first illustration in a *Collection of Emblemes*, where a candle burns atop a skull (see *plate 8*).[27] In the second of the quotations, from Act II, Death is placed in the less familiar rôle as a longed-for friend, a usage I shall consider presently. The third instance, from Act III, portrays Death in his usual guise as the destroyer of mortal things. This theme is common, particularly in church and church-yard depictions of the dance of death. For example, in the dance of death tableaux of the Cimetière des Innocents de Paris, the most famous burial place in sixteenth century Europe, one of the panels depicted a king and an emperor remonstrating with Death. Powerful rulers and monarchs they may be but Death is unimpressed: "Vous, roi, avec votre habit doré . . ." La Mort tells the king, "À la Mort vous n'avez pas pensé."[28] This is not a charge of which Richard is guilty for he retains a remarkably morbid and reflective disposition throughout the play. Even so, when Death finally visits him in the last act his exclamation, "How now . . .?" suggests a measure of surprise that even prolonged contemplation could not obviate. Death may be academicized and rationalized but nothing can make it routine.

It has become customary to remark upon Richard's strange "victory" in the closing scenes of the play. Harold F. Folland believes that "Richard, behind and through his apparently helpless self-dramatization, continues to fight his case against Bolingbroke so as to achieve a moral victory which has enduring political consequences. And in passing the royal power on to Henry, Richard subtly alters its character by dimming its numinous light."[29] Lois Potter is of the view that, even in death, "Richard dominates the scene in his silence as he had dominated it before with words."[30] More recently, William B. Bache has offered a succinct summary of the shift in the play's moral perspective: "The action of *Richard II* begins as it does because of the murder of Gloucester; the play draws to a close with the murder of 'another' Gloucester. The play begins with Bolingbroke confronting Richard; the play ends with Richard, in his coffin, confronting Henry."[31]

The case for Richard's triumph is particularly persuasive in the deposition scene where the unseated king consistently trumps awkward attempts to discredit him, responding to his captivity with a blend of defiance and wit:

> *K. Richard.* God save the King! Will no man say amen?
> Am I both priest and clerk? Well then, amen.
> (IV.i.172-3)

> *Bullingbrook.*   Name it, fair cousin.
> *K. Richard.* "Fair cousin"? I am greater than a king;
> For when I was a king my flatterers
> Were then but subjects; being now a subject,
> I have a king here to my flatterer.
> Being so great, I have no need to beg.
> (IV.i.304-9)

> *Bullingbrook.* Go some of you, convey him to the Tower.
> *K. Richard.* O, good! convey! Conveyers are you all,
> That rise thus nimbly by a true king's fall.
> (IV.i.316-18)

Lurking on the periphery of Bullingbrook's new court, Richard scoffs at its pomp, ridicules its usurped authority, deflects its censure. In a scene that witnesses the "official" transference of power or, in loyalist terms, the ceremonial fall of paradise, the significance of Richard's presence to the rebel assemblage perhaps has something in common with Hans Holbein's smiling, skeletal Death shadowing Adam in the world after the Fall (see *plate 6*). Within two scenes, Bullingbrook must endure the indignity of an abortive attempt on his life and, a scene after that, the irony of the Duchess of York's grateful praise: "A god on earth thou art" (V.iii.136). If murderous conspiracy aimed at his life proves nothing else, it demonstrates that Bullingbrook is in no way immune to the machinations of this world, lacking both the omnipotent power and the immortality of the Duchess' "god on earth." Standing in his foe's court, mocking his majesty with world-weary humor, Richard, like a skeleton of former glory, both reminds us of what Bullingbrook is yet to become and figuratively, as Death the antic jester, confirms an Hebraic scheme of the fallen world — a scheme once muted by the repetitive, death-defying greatness of English heroism. Bullingbrook may applaud his new order but it is one shadowed by grim inversions and disturbing innuendoes.

Richard's death is not least amongst these. His final moments are a frenetic far cry from the gentle expiry of old Lear or the verbose passing of Othello. The dramatic scenario Richard had constructed for himself at III.ii.160-70 finds a grim fulfillment in a murder that, for its violent movement, has much in common with the deformed animation of the dance of death itself. Here, in the play's penultimate act, the murderers and Exton rush into the king's Pomfret cell:

> *The murderers [Exton and servants] rush in [armed].*
> *King Richard.* How now, what means death in this rude assault?
> Villain, thy own hand yields thy death's instrument.
> *[Snatches an axe from a Servant and kills him.]*
> Go thou and fill another room in hell.
> 　　*[Kills another.] Here Exton strikes him down.*
> That hand shall burn in never-quenching fire
> That staggers thus my person.
> 　　　　　　　　　(V.v.105-9)

Holinshed provides a number of different accounts of King Richard's death, including the rumor that he "was tantalized with food and starved to death."[32] Shakespeare selects the story that he was murdered by Sir Pierce of Exton, quite possibly because this provided him with an opportunity to create on stage the theatrical emulation of a familiar funerary emblem. Hitherto, Richard's attitude had been a consummate illustration of *de contemptu mundi*: he has ridiculed Bullingbrook's court, engaged its niceties with mortuary humor, reflected calmly on his own mortality. But, however much revelatory self-understanding he has achieved, it is apparently insufficient to mitigate the surprise and alarm of death itself. "How now, what means death in this rude assault?" he cries. Richard's shock at the arrival of his killers is reminiscent of the *danse macabre* victims in any number of mural or folio presentations — some of whom struggle desperately to elude Death's grasp but none of whom succeeds. So it is with Richard. He puts up a brave fight but, inevitably, the emissaries of Death triumph.

Shakespeare's theatre at this moment animates a static icon of mortality, the dance of death *topos*, transforming its latent energy into the kinetics of dramatic action. He creates a theatrical emblem that draws for inspiration not only on the visual impersonation of the *danse macabre* but on the allegorical substance of that tradition as well. What we see, then, is both dramatic spectacle and embedded meaning. We are at once reminded of the dance of death and enriched by the ancillary associations (death as a leveler; the transience of mortality) that such recollection bestows. It is, however, more than a simple mimetic process. Richard *kills* two of his attackers, a course uncharted in the standard iconographies of death. Shakespeare tailors the familiar image to suit his theatrical designs, at once validating the idea, expressed by Richard himself, that not even a king is immune to the onslaught of death and, at the same time, signaling the admirable vigor of a weak monarch who unexpectedly emerges as a kind of everyman battling against the cyclical processes of mortality. For all the foibles of his character and the shadows of his past, the manipulation of the final visual impression of Richard's life lends to it a sense of heroic mortality. In the battle for life in the Pomfret cell, and in the stark symbol of the coffin in the last scene of the play, Shakespeare's visual designs become theatrical emblems in a vast and tragic mythology of English paradise lost.

Significantly, Richard's final words assert a decidedly Biblical disjunction between spirit and flesh:

> Mount, mount, my soul! thy seat is up on high,
> Whilst my gross flesh sinks downward, here to die.
> [*Dies.*]
> (V.v.111-12)

In *The Faerie Queene*, Spenser repudiates "fleshly might, / And vaine assurance of mortality" which all too readily "yeelds by and by, / Or from the field most cowardly doth fly" (I.x.1). A concise aphorism, unambiguously opposing the material and the spiritual. By contrast, the sense of English paradise, discussed in Chapter 2, saw a conjunction of the "earthly" and the "spiritual," redefining the latter term as part of an anglicized encomium of heroic Englishness. Richard's final words, shadowing Spenser's reasoning, pointedly disavow the correlation, asserting an antithesis of flesh and spirit, and implicitly repudiating the idea that there is anything paradisial about Bullingbrook's England.

* * * * *

The desire for death as an escape from the toils of life is a familiar refrain of Elizabethan and Jacobean tragedy, and appears widely in Shakespeare's canon. Valentine, in *Two Gentlemen of Verona*, sees little point in life without his beloved Silvia and vows to "attend on death" (III.i.186) and not to fly from him. "I crave death more willingly than mercy," says Angelo in *Measure for Measure*, "'Tis my deserving, and I do entreat it" (V.i.476-7). Antony promises to be "A bridegroom in my death, and run into't / As to a lover's bed" (*Antony and Cleopatra* IV.xiv.100-1). And Roderigo, in *Othello*, advises that "It is silliness to live when to live is torment; and then have we a prescription to die, when death is our physician" (I.iii.308-10). Angelo's allusion is the odd one out here. He perceives death as a mere state of being, a simple antithesis to "life." The other three references are more clearly in the personified and animated tradition of the *danse macabre*. Valentine and Antony are willing attendants on Death; and Roderigo draws on the idea of Death as a physician or apothecary, a function recited in some continental emblematizations.

There is, though, an obvious distinction between a casual allusion to Death and a coherent development of the dance of death *topos* within the dramatic framework of a given play. Marston's *The Malcontent* offers an illustration of purposeful and sustained experimentation with images of the "living dead" and with the theatricalization of the *danse macabre* itself (V.ii.). There is coherent patterning, too, in Beaumont and Fletcher's *The Knight of the Burning Pestle* which avoids the common *danse macabre* motif of Death as the cruel huntsmen, caricaturing him, instead, as a mischievous street urchin (V.iii.155), or positioning him as a much-desired friend:

> thou that art
> The end of all, and the sweete rest of all;
> Come, come ô death, bring me to thy peace,
> And blot out all the memory I nourish
> Both of my father and my cruell friend!
>
> (Luce, IV.iv.5-9)

Luce's understanding is not at all constructed from the traditions of Death as a terrorizing monstrosity. On the contrary, Death is, for her, the sweet emissary of rest and the merciful obliterator of painful memory. This function is something akin to that articulated by the Queen in *Richard II* when she longs for Death "Who gently would dissolve the bands of life" (II.ii.71). The sense of dissolution is pertinent to both women. Luce's image of memory blotted out suggests the dissipation of consciousness, the "blot" of memory that expands to the point of ultimate dilution, of non-entity. The Queen's metaphor is one envisaging the diffusion of substance, the melting of the bands of life. Death, for these characters, is a state of "not-knowing" and "not-feeling," a state of nothingness.

Like Beaumont and Fletcher, Shakespeare is drawing on a less familiar tradition of the dance of death which forwards Death as the courteous assistant, helping those who wish to approach the end of life to break the ties of mortality and to move into a happier domain. In this capacity, skeletal Death appears like a benign guardian, gently assisting the departure from life. Holbein's thirty-third print in *Imagines Mortis* (1545), "The Old Man," exemplifies this tradition. Here, Death, looking decidedly sympathetic, helps an old man in his walk to the grave. The old man's left foot hovers on the edge of a gaping hole, and a further stride will take him into it. Death's brow looks furrowed in sympathy; and although he holds a musical instrument he resists playing it, his right hand, instead, acting as a crutch for his charge. There is none of the grinning triumphalism that typifies Holbein's other *danse macabre* figures. Instead,

we have Death the sympathetic manservant. That, at least, is one
interpretation. It could just be that Death's sympathy is merely a ruse,
and that the old man, looking into Death's compassionate eye-sockets, is
distracted at the very moment he is about to plunge into the yawning
abyss of the grave.[33]

There are less ambiguous examples. A thoroughly unthreatening
Death figure is that in the eighty-ninth emblem of Georgette de Montenay's
Emblematvm Christianorvm Centvria (*plate 23*).[34] Here, an affable
skeleton offers a helping hand to an old man who willingly steps forth
from out of a symbolically hollow world:

> De grand desir d'aller bien tost a Dieu,
> Cestuy se void presque sorty du monde:
> Crainte de mor en son endroit n'a lieu,
> Ainsi qu'elle a au coeur sale & immonde.

The "grand desir" to be with God turns Death into a charming accomplice
in the escape from this world to the next. The comforting, dainty hand
he lends to the old man casts him in the guise of a carer rather than of a
demonic slayer of mortality. His delicate grasp supports the volunteer,
enabling him to step safely out of the orb. A Latin motto, "desiderans
dissolvi" (the desire of dissolution), is written in the clouds above the
old man's head. There is nothing fearful or gloating about this species of
Death. On the contrary, his coming is to be wished for.

The idea of dissolution, evidenced in de Montenay's print and
articulated by Luce in *The Knight of the Burning Pestle* and the Queen in
Richard II, is an intriguing one. Clearly, in each case dissolution is
viewed as desirable — but dissolution into *what*? De Montenay's woodcut
leaves us in no doubt about her understanding of "dissolution." On the
left of the print a road leads up a mountainside into the clouds of heaven.
There is here a clear and hopeful eschatology of the afterlife, the promise
of the beatific presence after death — a possibility confirmed by the
accompanying verse. But Luce and Richard's Queen live in dramatic
landscapes which offer only ambivalent assurance of life beyond the
grave, and their words do not countenance such a hope. Shakespeare's
theatre, like that of Beaumont and Fletcher, seems to have been resolutely
vague in its speculations about what it is, exactly, that life dissolves into.
Even Hamlet, compulsively morbid and one of Shakespeare's most
intellectually responsive characters, can hope only that

> this too too [solid] flesh would melt
> Thaw, and resolve itself into a dew!
>
> (*Hamlet* I.ii.129-30)

However much we construe into Renaissance notions of "dew" (and there is, admittedly, a deal to be said on that matter), Hamlet's comment on the world after life has "melted" away can hardly be characterized as illuminating.

One character, though, who does have a very clear image of what she would like to happen after death is Constance, in *King John*. Supposing that her son, Arthur, has been murdered, she longs for amiable Death in a manner considerably more precise than Luce or the Queen:

> Death, death. O amiable lovely death!
> Thou odoriferous stench! sound rottenness!
> Arise forth from the couch of lasting night,
> Thou hate and terror to prosperity,
> And I will kiss thy detestable bones,
> And put my eyeballs in thy vaulty brows,
> And ring these fingers with thy household worms,
> And stop this gap of breath with fulsome dust,
> And be a carrion monster like thyself.
> Come, grin on me, and I will think thou smil'st,
> And buss thee as thy wife. Misery's love,
> O, come to me!
>
> (III.iv.25-36)

Roland Mushat Frye regards this as "one of the most gruesome treatments of Death and the Woman"[35] in literature but, to me, the victim's consensual extravagance serves to reduce this to pathos (or even bathos) rather than horror. As in de Montenay's emblem, Death becomes a cherished friend whose grisly smile is as welcome as his deathly stench. In her promise to "buss thee as thy wife," Constance also touches upon the iconographical tradition of Death as a bridegroom. Theodore de Bry's *Emblemata* offers a *danse macabre* print in which Death's bride is portrayed as an obviously bashful skeleton, endorsing the notion of Death as a faithful lover meeting his paramour at the appointed time of union.[36] But Constance's construction is unusual. It inverts the customary protocol of Death summoning the doomed. Instead, as with Luce in *The Knight of the*

Burning Pestle, it is the doomed who summon Death, urging the amiable ruffian to "Arise forth from the couch of lasting night," rather like the skeletal emissaries of Michael Wolgemut's 1493 woodcut. The images of mortal decay (stench, rottenness, bones, worms, eye sockets) reflect the opposites of life and compound for Constance an extravagant antithesis to living existence. She even tells Death that she wishes to be "a carrion monster like thyself," visiting death upon others as death has been visited, she believes, upon her son Arthur.

This is a sharp departure from the sentiments of the emblem books. Assuredly, the rejection of life in English iconography in the fifty year period running from the 1580s varies considerably. Geffrey Whitney (1586), for example, depicts a well-dressed man striding purposefully away from a globe of the world upon which the names of the continents are written.[37] Francis Quarles (1634), by contrast, represents physical life as a skeleton in a bird cage:

> My soul is like a Bird, my flesh the cage
> Wherein she wears her weary pilgrimage
> Of hours, as few as evil, daily fed
> With sacred Wine, and Sacramental Bread;
> The keyes that lock her in, and let her out,
> Are Birth and Death. . . .[38]

But, despite differences of approach and visualization, the significance of the icons remains consistent, and may be summarized by the motto appended to the print of Whitney's striding man: "Adve deceiptfull worlde, thy pleasures I detest: / Now, others with thy showes delude; my hope in heauen doth rest" (p. 225).

Constance, though, is moving in a substantially different direction here. She wants to *be* a carrion monster, a death dancer. Not for her the verdant fields and aromatic flowers of heaven. No. With a worm circling her finger as a wedding ring, she desires to marry Death, dust and all, and become part of his grinning, grimacing world. It is not exactly clear what Constance hopes to gain by this, except perhaps the dubious satisfaction of inflicting grief upon others in the way that grief has been inflicted upon her. There is certainly life beyond her death but it is not the spiritual life suggested by de Montenay and Quarles. For her, "life" returns as a monstrosity. Before death, she was misery's prisoner; after death, she proposes to become misery's harbinger. Her mental state is parlous indeed — a condition King Philip is quick to recognize:

Look who comes here! a grave unto a soul;
Holding th' eternal spirit, against her will,
In the vil[e] prison of afflicted breath.
                                        (III.iv.17-19)

The allusion is to the familiar emblem motif of the soul as a prisoner of
the physical being. A woodcut in Francis Quarles' *Emblemes* (1634)
depicts a despondent soul imprisoned within the rib cage of a smiling
skeleton.[39] And in the wonderfully emblematized opening to Kyd's *The
Spanish Tragedy*, Andrea's ghost remembers "When this eternal substance
of my soul / Did live imprisoned in my wanton flesh" (I.i.1-2).

After Constance's intimations of post-mortality, the dance of death
returns in varied guises to the dramatic terrain of *King John*.
Faulconbridge twice uses it as a sign of superlative English soldiership
(II.i.350-5 and 455-60); and, in the opening scene of the final act, there
are two more engaging references:

                         and in his forehead sits
      A bare-ribb'd death, whose office is this day
      To feast upon whole thousands of the French.
                           (Faulconbridge of John, V.ii.176-8)

      Have I not hideous death within my view,
      Retaining but a quantity of life,
      Which bleeds away even as a form of wax
      Resolveth from his figure 'gainst the fire?
                           (Melune, V.iv.22-5)

Faulconbridge's claim that King John has metamorphosed into a kind of
feasting Death-figure is an absurd over-statement — but it is useful as an
ironic counterpoint to John's predicament a few scenes later where Death
is recast as a predator besieging the monarch's life. Melune's image of
hideous Death advancing upon him, as life melts away like a wax figure
dissolving before a flame, is more interesting. Whereas Luce and
Richard's Queen see dissolution as an intellectual process, a kind of
abstract euphemism to compass the transition from life to death, Melune
reports on the actual physical process of death (the blood that "bleeds
away"), paralleling it with the idea of a melting figure. Death's response
is reactive rather than proactive. As life fades, so Death comes closer —

a little like Tamburlaine's Death who advances on the dying emperor
when he is not looking but retreats when seen (*Tamburlaine, Part 2,*
V.iii.69-72).[40] In both cases, Death is not the typically cavorting ruffian
of Holbein's series, seizing his victim gleefully and dragging him off.
He is, rather, a scavenger Death who arrives when there is carrion to be
had but has no warrant to forage living flesh.

The permutations of the *danse macabre* in *King John* are useful
preparations in advance of the play's final scene for which are reserved
the most acrid icons of dissolving mortality. And, as in *Richard II*, the
concluding minutes of *King John* present us with a theatrical emblem of
the dance of death. The king has been poisoned and it is reported that
Death is preying on both his flesh and his mind:

> Death, having prey'd upon the outward parts,
> Leaves them invisible, and his siege is now
> Against the mind, the which he pricks and wounds
> With many legions of strange fantasies. . . .
>
> (Prince Henry, V.vii.15-17)

Then the afflicted monarch himself is borne into the room by attendants.
He is seated in a chair, as are many of the royal personages of Holbein's
dance of death series. Surrounded by helpless courtiers and servants,
and yet begging vainly for help, the king articulates the final agonized
moments of his life, using the figurative diction of emblem book verse.
His bowels, he says, "crumble up to dust" (V.vii.31) and he is consumed
by shriveling heat:

> I am a scribbled form, drawn with a pen
> Upon a parchment, and against this fire
> Do I shrink up.
>
> (lines 32-4).

An interesting analogy, recalling Edward the Black Prince's comment in
Edward III when, seeing a mortally wounded compatriot, he asks who
has "writ that note of death in Audley's face?" (IV.ix.20).[41] And
suggestive, too, of those other scribbled forms drawn on emblem book
parchment. John's understanding of his own diminution is remarkable
for its lucidity. The end of mortality seems to endow so many of
Shakespeare's characters with highly expressive qualities of verbalization

and perception, and similar largess is accorded to John and Melune. Melune, while watching himself die, is able to tie in the flow of blood from his body with the double notion of melting wax and the "candle of life," a familiar motif of human impermanence in the emblem books. John, his body ravaged by poison, is still capable of transfiguring the "fire" consuming him within into an image of parchment paper shriveling against the heat of flame. These literary achievements, in the face of imminent personal demise, are quite extraordinary. And, I think, deliberate. Both men define the dissolution of a material figure — a "form of wax" for Melune; a "scribbled form" for John. The processes of that dissolution are absolute and irreversible, a precise shadowing of the end of mortal being. Absolute, because neither man appears to suppose that anything lies beyond melted wax or paper seared to ashes; irreversible, because the uniqueness of each artifact is irreplaceable. The sense of destruction, then, is a humanized one, compassing not simply the loss of physical mortality but also the uniqueness of being, the idiosyncrasy of individuality. The human race will endure, perhaps prosper, but the individualities of Melune and of John will be lost forever.

This extreme individualization of the play's tragedy is sustained in John's continuing commentary on the dissolution of his life. Tormented as his mind may be, his affirmation of the certitude of death recalls the dance of death's infallible grasp. His sentence, he says, is "unreprievable."

> Within me is a hell, and there the poison
> Is as a fiend confin'd to tyrannize
> On unreprievable condemned blood.
>   (lines 46-8)

There is here the gratuitous violence of the *danse macabre*, the unnecessary tyranny of victory. King John's fate is sealed; his condemned life "unreprievable." Still Death tortures him. It is not enough that a man should merely die. In the rather crude manner of the early *danse macabre* plays, the brutal lesson of mortal fragility must also be seared on the minds of those who watch. That Shakespeare intended his version of John's predicament to represent the ultimate extremity of suffering may be deduced from the relationship of this episode to its source in *The Troublesome Reign of King John*. Paola Pugliatti notices that, while in the original John can glean some comfort from the return of rebellious barons and the promise that Prince Henry will be crowned king soon,

"Shakespeare's John dies without hope: the last words he hears are the news that the Bastard somewhat ungenerously gives him about the armed approach of the Dolphin in a situation that appears to be hopeless for the English."[42]

In his last mortal words, Shakespeare's King John describes himself as "a module of confounded royalty," a neat conspectus of the commonplace motif that Death, the great leveler, will bring even the high and mighty to book. The words that follow affirm the aphorism succinctly: Salisbury says simply "But now a king, now thus" (V.vi.66); Prince Henry offers a phrase of similar equipoise: "this was now a king and now is clay" (line 69); and Faulconbridge can only ask bemusedly "Art thou gone so?" (line 70) as if somehow he thought kings were immune to mortal vagaries. One curious point, though. We might have thought that King John's suffering through poisoning would have urged him to the same conclusion Constance reached three acts earlier — namely, that death is an end to life's misery and should therefore be embraced. He expresses no such view. And while Richard, that most excellent contemplator of death, may be infused with alarm when the gory vizard of Death reveals itself at the end of *Richard II*, he is still able to die with the certainty of heaven on his lips. King John, though, can find no such peace. He clings to tenuous life and this world as keenly as ever he did, lamenting bitterly that only a "thread, one little hair" secures him to the pulse of mortality. For him, as for the typical *danse macabre* victim, there is no comforting vision of heaven at hand when skeletal Death approaches. For him, the circuit of mortal life is everything. The "nothingness" of death that Luce and Richard's Queen desire so urgently is, for John, a prospect of appalling and unmitigable loss.

* * * * *

In sixteenth century picture and word, Death was familiarly linked with soldiership. Many examples are extant. Frighteningly uncongenial is Georgette de Montenay's skeletal emissary in *Emblematvm Chrstianorvm Centvria* as he gleefully lynches a soldier.[43] Vincentio Saviolo's *His Practise. In two Bookes* (1595), on the subject of single combat and honorable quarrels, reveals a print of a ragged Death emissary looking at a proud knight on horseback and pointing to the skeleton of a soldier lying on the ground nearby: "O Wormes Meate. . ." he yells out, "Why Art Thou So Insolent."[44] Examples of Death as a soldier are also numerous. In Guillaume de la Perrière's *La Morosophie*, Death is armed with an infantry lance as he weighs the accessories of the rich man and the poor man. The lance, or javelin, had powerful associations with soldiership in the late Medieval and Renaissance eras. The supremacy of feudal cavalry had been shattered by the English invention of the long bow, a device capable of piercing armor at six hundred yards. First used decisively at the Battle of Falkirk (1298), its deployment was perfected to devastating effect by Edward III at Crecy and Poitiers.[45] As a counter to the long bow, lightly armored foot soldiers carrying lances proved themselves superior to cavalry, offering the advantage of mobility, furtiveness and camouflage.

No doubt, the idea of Death as a lance-bearing soldier, fast-moving and stealthy, recommended itself to the emblematists. At any rate, the characteristics are indicative of skeletal Death in a range of emblematic representations, but particularly in Holbein's series where Death is occasionally portrayed as stalking the mortal world, awaiting his moment, or, as in "The Knight," driving his lance through the back of a surprised adversary. It finds further forceful expositions in the prints of Gabriel Simeoni, a Florentine whose *Pvrtratvres Or Emblemes* was published in London in 1591, on the cusp of Shakespeare's career. In a print that bears the motto "The wicked is moued to mercie with no entretie," a Death soldier, bearing a lance which is raised and poised to strike, is about to execute a prisoner *(plate 24)*.[46] The victim in question appears to be a captive soldier, a conclusion suggested by his military-style tunic. Simeoni's Death soldier, like de la Perrière's menacing leveler, and Holbein's back-lancing killer constitutes the unstoppable warrior, the ultimate adversary — the Death soldier.

The Death soldier motif has already been mooted in relation to English soldiership in *Henry V*, and he is envisioned, as well, as the siegeman of *Richard II* who bores through the king's "castle wall." He is present, too, in at least one Roman play. The hero of *Coriolanus*, Caius Marcius, is consistently characterized in terms of exceptional mortality. Brutus reports that, being moved, Marcius "will not spare to gird the gods" (I.i.256) and later rebukes the hero for speaking to the people "As if you were a god, to punish" (III.i.81). Cominius paints a picture of supreme warriorship: "He is their god; he leads them like a thing / Made by some other deity than Nature, / That shapes man better" (IV.vi.90-2). The association is not always celebrative and is subject to some criticism and even burlesque but the process of the play increasingly aggrandizes

Marcius' military stature to the point where he is perceived as irresistible and supernatural. And, to be more specific, Mars-like. While Shakespeare is able to draw a distinction in desirability between the English Mars and the Roman Mars in the second tetralogy, there can be no doubt that in the setting of Classical Rome, Classical Mars must reign supreme.[47] Not only does Coriolanus demonstrate the impetuosity, zeal, disdain of peace, and blood-lust of the Roman deity but in battle and distress he is apt to invoke the name of the god (at I.iv.10 and V.vi.99). On two further occasions, he is explicitly linked to Mars. Marcius' greatest foe, Aufidius, refers to him, in awe, as "thou Mars" (IV.v.118); and a servingman describes him as the "heir to Mars" (IV.v.192). Not all that surprising, given that Mars was the god of soldiers.

What has this to do with the idea of the dance of death? Well, one answer is that Renaissance literature commonly associated the warrior-god Mars with Death. Richard Linche's truncated 1595 translation of Vincenzo Cartari's *Le imagini de i Dei gli Antichi* (1556) offers a grotesque description of the figure of Death in the palace of Mars:

> wherevpon a stately altar, he [i.e. Death] was offering
> sacrifices in goblets made with the skuls of men, and filled
> vp euen to the brim with humane bloud; which oblation
> was consecrated to god Mars, with coales of fire (which
> set on flame the sacrifice) fetcht from many Citties, Townes
> and Holds, burnt and ruinated by tyrannie of the Warres.[48]

The statue of Mars at Hampton Court Palace reveals a death's head skull prominently on the war god's shield. In *Coriolanus*, Marcius, too, is quick to forward himself as the harbinger of death:

> Would the nobility lay aside their ruth
> And let me use my sword, I'd make a quarry
> With thousands of these quarter'd slaves, as high
> As I could pick my lance.
>   (I.i.197-200)

It is interesting that he uses the words "sword" and "lance" here together. The sword is his instrument of death, as we might expect of a patrician Roman; the lance is the "quantifier" of death. The number of people he would like to kill, he suggests, would make a pile as high as he could throw ("pick") his lance. There is no sense of uncertainty about this. Those he has identified *will* die until the quota is complete — escape from Death, in the tradition of the *danse macabre*, will be impossible.

These inferences of Death warriorship consolidate into a stronger identification two scenes later when his mother, Volumnia, aligns him with the Death-mower archetype:

> His bloody brow
> With his mail'd hand then wiping, forth he goes,
> Like to a harvest-man that's task'd to mow
> Or all or lose his hire.
>
> (I.iii.34-7)

The unrecanting mower figure is no stranger either to Shakespeare or to Renaissance iconography. In *Henry V*, the king describes how his Death soldiers will roam "with conscience wide as hell, mowing like grass / Your fresh fair virgins and your flow'ring infants" (III.iii.13-14). A fifteenth century French text, *Eruditorium penitentiale*, shows a gathering of Death figures in macabre gardening poses.[49] One holds a spade, another grasps a scythe. Jacob Wimpheling, in *Adolescentia* (1500), chooses to portray Death as a skeletal figure, swinging a scythe in a grassy graveyard.[50] These images, too, are evident in the Beram dance of death pageant where a scythe-bearing death leads off a vintner.

What, in fact, Volumnia is saying about her son when she compares him "to a harvest-man that's task'd to mow / Or all or lose his hire" is that he is an indiscriminate and unswerving killer. Rather like Simeoni's Death soldier, he "is moued to mercie with no entretie." This may not constitute wickedness, in Simeoni's sense of the word, but it certainly speaks to Marcius' Death-like heartlessness on the field of battle, a quality echoed, as we have seen, in Holbein's cut of "The Knight" where Death, having come up behind the knight, brutally dispatches him.[51] The link between Marcius and the *danse macabre* is soon made wholly explicit.

> *Menenius.* Now it's twenty seven [ie wounds], every gash
> was an enemy's grave. [*A shout and flourish.*] Hark, the trumpets.
> *Volumnia.* These are the ushers of Marcius: before him
> he carries noise, and behind him he leaves tears:
> Death, that dark spirit, in 's nervy arm doth lie,

Which, being advanc'd, declines, and then men die.
A sennet. Trumpets sound.

(*Coriolanus* II.i.155-61)

Before him he carries noise, Volumnia tells us. After him, he leaves tears. When his arm declines, she says, men die. Even she seems slightly unnerved by "Death, that dark spirit" that seems to power her son's killing-arm. We have, in Volumnia's description, the topography of the dance of death: the blaring of trumpets, recalling one of the musical instruments most commonly carried by Death in the emblem books; the sound and the fury of his presence; the fateful and irresistible doom of his stroke; the sense of blind and unstoppable mission.

These images of Death as a life-cropping warrior are attached, as well, to Shakespeare's other superlative soldiers. Faulconbridge, that consummate English warrior in *King John*, twice invokes the name of Death as a soldier:

O now doth Death line his dead chaps with steel,
The swords of soldiers are his teeth, his fangs,
And now he feasts, mousing the flesh of men,
In undetermin'd differences of kings.
Why stand these royal fronts amazed thus?
Cry "havoc!" kings.

(II.i.352-7)

Here's a stay [of battle]
That shakes the rotten carcass of old Death
Out of his rags!

(II.i.455-7)

On first appraisal, these do not appear as particularly endearing portraitures of Death. Even so, it is clear that Faulconbridge exudes a certain enchantment with the notion of Death as a soldier, invoking battlefield carnage in Act II and (erroneously, as I have suggested) comparing King John to a Death figure when addressing the French in the last act.

So, too, in *Coriolanus* the notion of Marcius as a Death soldier is signified as celebratory, if a little frightening even to his mother. Yet, having encouraged this mystique around his hero, it is indicative of Shakespeare's method that, at the last, he reverses the iconographic significances. Having been carefully positioned as a Martian god and Death soldier, Marcius finds himself abruptly divested of immortal trappings. It is, if you like, a process of humanization, a series of emblematic tableaux that remind the hero, and ourselves as the audience, that the mortal world is marked by, well, mortality. First, Aufidius strips from Marcius the accoutrements of deification: "Name not the god, thou boy of tears!" (V.vi.100). It is, to be fair, the insult of "boy" that most offends Marcius, and rouses him to a boastful account of the deaths he has wreaked upon the Volscian nation. This is not good policy because it reminds those present of his rôle as the all-consuming Death soldier, and by so doing Marcius "commits a kind of suicide"[52]:

> *All the People.* Tear him to pieces. Do it presently!—
> He kill'd my son!— My daughter!— He kill'd my
> cousin Marcus. He kill'd my father!
>   (V.vi.120-2)

Those present articulate his rôle as the universal slayer of humankind and, spurred on by the conspirators, bay for his blood. His mortality exposed, even the Death soldier himself must die. A Lord shouts out "Peace, ho! No outrage — peace!" (line 125) but the rabble advances. Shakespeare's text neatly counterpoints the cries of "kill" with those of "hold," and between them, in this midst of a frenzied struggle between life and death, Marcius perishes:

> *All Conspirators.* Kill, kill, kill, kill, kill him!
> *The Conspirators draw and kill Martius, who falls;*
> *Aufidius stands on him.*
> *Lords.*   Hold, hold, hold, hold!
>   (V.vi.131-2)

The tussle for Marcius' life, like that between many a *danse macabre* victim and his skeletal foe, has proved futile.

On the stage, the visual image of Marcius' engulfment, as sudden as it is spectacular, presents a truly shocking emblem of life's transience. The man who was wont to battle whole armies is dispatched in a trice. Superbly alive one moment; no more than "Wormes Meate" an instant later. Nor should we ignore the triumphalism of Aufidius as he stands upon the corpse of Marcius. Holbein's forty-second woodcut in the dance of death series, entitled "The Soldier," reveals skeletal Death in combat with a desperate infantryman. Instead of a sword, Death wields a human bone high above his head, its fatal force about to decline on his adversary. Beneath Death's feet, the bodies of the dead are trampled unceremoniously; and in the distance, a second dance of death figure leads an army into battle, banging a drum as he does so. In *Coriolanus*, too, the conqueror of the Death soldier becomes, in a poignant and powerful visual icon, the spontaneous figure of Death himself, crudely celebrating his victory in a hideous desecration of mortality. A Lord, the representative of mortal authority, commands him to get off Marcius' body, and Aufidius, apparently filled with remorse, immediately does so.[53] Twice in the lines that follow the idea that Coriolanus must be taken off for burial is iterated, echoing the sense of the *danse macabre* victim being conveyed to oblivion. "Beat thou the drum" (V.vi.149) Aufidius commands. And, in the final emblem of the play, Marcius' body is marched off stage, the drum marking its irrevocable journey to the grave. This, though, is not the zealous death drum of "The Soldier" or "The Bones of All Men." This is a more muted drum, one that encompasses both the splendor of mortality and the sad certainty of its passing.

* * * * *

Nigel Llewellyn has discussed at some length the emphasis placed by the English Church, both before and after the Reformation, on the need for "spiritual preparation."[54] Reflection on death, underpinned by a vast array of images and artifacts, served to emphasize the existence of God's grander design, a mysterious design, at times, as the culmination of *Romeo and Juliet* might suggest but, for all its lack of transparency, no less certain or valid. Amongst all the moralizing imagery endorsed and promoted by the Church, and embraced by poets and artists alike from Holbein in the sixteenth century to Rowlandson in the early 1800s, the dance of death, Llewellyn suggests, was the most powerful image in the popular consciousness (p. 19).

In *Hamlet*, Shakespeare may indeed be moving in a direction broadly parallel to church teachings on the meaning and learning potential of deathly consideration. Certainly, the thesis that contemplation of mortality can lead to a kind of calm and even understanding is stated in that play with greater confidence than it was in the more tentative denouement of

Romeo and Juliet. But in the three plays discussed in this chapter —
Richard II, King John, and *Coriolanus* — it is clear a process of
reconstruction is taking place and that Shakespeare, in each case, is moving
outside the normative parameters of church meaning and usage, and into
a more experimental domain. *Coriolanus* stands as the most challenging
and, perhaps, successful of these endeavors. Having ultimately balked
at the concept of the Death soldier in the second tetralogy, it took
Shakespeare almost a decade to return to the idea, transposing it from an
English into an Italian context and, curiously, finding its validity not in
success but in failure. The problem with the Death soldiers of *Henry V*
is that they become extra-human, conquering all before them and metamor-
phosing from men into monsters; the triumph of *Coriolanus* is,
paradoxically, that the superlative path of the Death soldier draws him
not to barbarity but to annihilation. However we idealize our heroes,
however we deify and eulogize them, it is the recognition of our common
mortality that fully binds them to us, and us to them.

Notes

1. See Emile Mâle, *L'Art Religieux de la fin du Moyen Âge en France* (Paris: Librairie Armand Colin, 1908), pp. 375-422.
2. Compare *Everyman* to the rather more rudimentary fourteenth century Latin versions of the *danse macabre*, such as that reproduced in Jozef Ijsewijn's article "A Latin Death-dance play of 1532," *Humanistica Lovaniensia: Journal of Neo-Latin Studies*, 18 (1969), pp. 77-94. See, also, Jane H. M. Taylor, "The Dialogues of the Dance of Death and the Limits of Late-Medieval Theatre," *Fifteenth Century Studies*, 16 (1990), pp. 215-32.
3. See James M. Clark, *The Dance of Death by Hans Holbein* (London: Phaidon Press, 1947), pp. 7-36.
4. The manuscript was authored by Guyot Marchant and is now housed in the Bibliothèque de Grenoble.
5. Clark, p. 8, also notes a dance of death series on the ribs of the choir vault at Rosslyn Church, near Edinburgh. There is, as well, an interesting wall painting at Charlwood Church, Surrey, of the celebrated tradition of "The Three Living and the Three Dead," in which three skeletal Death figures appear (but not in particularly animated guise).
6. The existence of a dance of death series at the Grove Chapel is considered by several commentators, including James M. Clark, *The Dance of Death by Hans Holbein*, pp. 7-36. Harry Morris, "The Dance of Death in Shakespeare," *Papers on Language and Literature*, 20 (1984), writes that "marginal notation made by the antiquary, John Stow, in his copy of Leland's *Itinerary*, refers to a Dance of Death in the guildhall chapel of Straford-on-Avon" (p. 16). M. D. Anderson, *History and Imagery in British Churches* (London: John Murray, 1995), is silent on the Grove Chapel issue in his discussion of the dance of death.
7. *Everyman*, ed. Geoffrey Cooper and Christopher Wortham (Nedlands: University of Western Australia Press, 1980).
8. Hartman Schedel, *Liber Chronicum* (Nuremberg: 1493). Sometimes known as the "Chronicle of Nuremberg."
9. *Danse Macabre* (Troyes, France: after 1500), leaves aii /b and aiii /a. Author unknown. The manuscript is housed in the Saxon State Library, Dresden, Germany.
10. Francis Beaumont, *The Knight of the Burning Pestle*, ed. Andrew Gurr (Berkeley and Los Angeles: The University of California Press, 1966).
11. Hans Holbein, *Imagines Mortis* (Lyon: Trechsel, 1545). The work was first published in 1538 by the Trechsel brothers in Lyon under the title *Les Simulachres & Historiees faces de la Mort, avtant elegammet pourtraictes, que artificiellement imaginées*. The 1545 and subsequent editions added further cuts to the original collection.

12. The 1545 edition, besides the original forty-one prints, contained as well a further twelve cuts, including: the Soldier, the Gambler, the Drunkard, the Fool, the Robber, the Blind Man, the Waggoner, and the Beggar. Holbein designed the prints but relied on the brilliant engraver, Lützelburger, to execute them. Lützelburger died in 1526, some twelve years before the work was published. Why Holbein delayed the printing of the manuscript for so long is still a matter of conjecture.

13. Edmund Spenser, *The Faerie Queene*, ed. Thomas P. Roche (Harmondsworth: Penguin Books, 1978).

14. William E. Engel, *Mapping Mortality: The Persistence of Memory and Melancholy in Early Modern England* (Amherst: University of Massachusetts Press, 1995), p. 83.

15. See Arthur B. Chamberlain, *Hans Holbein The Younger* (London: George Allen, 1913), II, p. 186.

16. Chamberlain, in *Hans Holbein The Younger* (London: George Allen, 1913), I, pp. 212-4, lists some of the many editions of the *Imagines Mortis* that appeared in various parts of Europe in the sixteenth century.

17. Clark, p. 32.

18. Clark, p. 32. Many such imitations are housed in Oxford University's Bodleian Library.

19. Hans Holbein, *The Images of the Old Testament* (Lyon: Johan Frellon, 1549). See Arthur Chamberlain, *Hans Holbein The Younger*, II, p. 186.

20. Significant, too, was the notion that (skeletal) Death was latent within every human being, a perspective encouraged by advances in medical science. Michael Neill, in *Issues of Death: Mortality and Identity in English Renaissance Tragedy* (Oxford: Clarendon Press, 1997), has made the point that "what the science of dissection ultimately seemed to disclose was nothing less than the 'original of Death'— the death that is always already inside us, its presence marked by the very structure that, in Banister's words [*Historie of Man, sucked from the sappe of the most approued Anathomistes* (London: 1578)], comprises 'the body's framework' or 'foundation'" (p. 133).

21. Andrew Willet, *Sacrorum Emblematum Centuria Una* (London: 1592), emblem 40.

22. Thomas Combe, trans, *Guillaume de la Perrière: The Theater of fine devices, containing an hundred morall emblemes* (London: 1593), emblem XXVII.

23. Douce's observation is noted in Matthew W. Black, ed., *A New Variorum Edition of Shakespeare: The Life and Death of King Richard the Second* (Philadelphia: Lippincott, 1955), p. 198. The issue is debatable.

24. Black also cites Collier as making the point that "death is represented as taking off the emperor's crown; and not sitting and keeping his court in it" (p. 198).

25. Morris, p. 20.
26. Judith Dundas in her essay "The Masks of Cupid and Death," *Comparative Drama*, 29 (1995), argues that this allusion ties in with Geffrey Whitney's Cupid and Death emblem (see *plate 12*), since Whitney uses the term "Iocosum" (= humorous) as part of his motto for the print (pp. 44-5). The relationship is somewhat tenuous since Whitney's "Iocosum" relates to the farcical nature of the arrow mix up, as Dundas herself acknowledges (p. 45), rather than to the character of Death himself.
27. George Wither, *A Collection of Emblemes, Ancient and Moderne (1635)*, ed. Rosemary Freeman (Columbia: University of South Carolina Press, 1975), p. 21.
28. From the Marchant ms., Bibliothèque de Grenoble, France.
29. Harold F. Folland, "King Richard's Pallid Victory," *Shakespeare Quarterly*, 24 (1973), p. 390.
30. Lois Potter, "The Antic Disposition of Richard II," *Shakespeare Survey*, 27 (1974), p. 41.
31. William B. Bache, *Design and Closure in Shakespeare's Major Plays: The Nature of Recapitulation* (New York: Peter Lang, 1991), p. 131.
32. See Geoffrey Bullough, *Narrative and Dramatic Sources of Shakespeare*, III (London: Routledge & Kegan Paul, 1960), p. 413.
33. Clark, p. 116, writes "Is he [Death] deluding his victim or assisting him on his last journey? Most authorities prefer the kindlier solution."
34. Roland Mushat Frye, *The Renaissance Hamlet: Issues and Responses in 1600* (Princeton: Princeton University Press, 1984), p. 350.
35. Georgette de Montenay, *Emblematvm Christianorvm Centvria* (1571, first publ.; Zurich, 1584), emblem LXXXIX, p. 89r.
36. Theodore de Bry, *Emblemata* (Frankfurt am Main: 1593), "Fui, non svm es, nõ eris" (no pagination).
37. Geffrey Whitney, *A Choice of Emblemes* (Leyden: Christopher Plantin, 1586), p. 225.
38. Francis Quarles, *Emblemes* (London: J. Williams, 1634), p. 285.
39. Quarles, p. 272.
40. Christopher Marlowe, *The Complete Plays*, ed. J. B. Steane (Harmondsworth: Penguin Books, 1973).
41. The version used is that in G. Blakemore Evans et al., eds., *The Riverside Shakespeare*, 2nd Ed. (Boston: Houghton Mifflin, 1997).
42. Paola Pugliatti, *Shakespeare the Historian* (New York: St. Martin's Press, 1996), p. 97.
43. De Montenay, p. 4r.
44. Vincentio Saviolo, *His Practise. In two Bookes. The first intreating of the vse of the Rapier and Dagger. The second, of Honour and Honourable Quarrels* (London: T. Scarlet for J. Wolfe, 1595), sig. K3r.

45. C. W. C. Oman has discussed the evolution of the long bow in his classic work *The Art of War in the Middle Ages* (1885, first publ.; Ithaca and London: Cornell University Press, 1993), pp. 116-51.

46. Simeoni, p. 364.

47. *Lemprière's Classical Dictionary of Proper Names mentioned in Ancient Authors*, ed. F. A. Wright (London: Routledge & Kegan Paul, 1978), "Mercury."

48. Richard Linche, *The Fovntaine of Ancient Fiction* (1599; facsimile rpt. New York & London: Garland Publishing, Inc., 1976), sigs. X1r-X1v.

49. *Eruditorium penitentiale* (Paris: Antoine Caillaut, 1480), no pagination.

50. Jacob Wimpheling, *Adolescentia* (Strasbourg: Martin Flach, 1500), no pagination.

51. "The Knight" is print 31 in Holbein's series. Clark, p. 115, writes of this print: "In this, his final battle, the Knight does not submit tamely to his fate, for he is a man of mettle. Crying out in his agony, he defends himself desperately to the last, striking at Death with his sword as long as his ebbing strength permits. But it is all in vain, for his dread adversary has driven the Knight's own lance through his coat of mail and administered the fatal blow."

52. William B. Bache and Vernon P. Loggins, *Shakespeare's Deliberate Art* (Lanham, New York, & London: The University Press of America, 1996), p. 132.

53. Michael Neill suggests that Aufidius' praise may well be disingenuous: "what, after all, can we make of a tribute to heroic fame contrived by a man whose own actions appear to have destroyed the last remaining shreds of those values on which it might rest?" (p. 292).

54. Nigel Llewellyn, *The Art of Death: Visual Culture in the English Death Ritual c. 1500 - c. 1800* (London: Reaktion Books, in association with the Victoria and Albert Museum, 1991), p. 19.

Chapter 7

ຂ)ལ

Epilogue

Anyone interested in the visual humor of the Middle Ages should visit St. Peter and St. Paul's Church in Chaldon, Surrey, just south of London. On entering, the visitor's eye is immediately drawn to the altar and Medieval font, showered as they are by shards of light from ancient glass in the windows behind them. Then, turning to leave, the modern pilgrim, like his counterpart a thousand years ago, is shocked by a stunning vision of heaven and hell which looms high and vast out of the dimness of the back wall. It is a riveting spectacle, a scheme of angels and devils, saints and sinners, unqualified bliss and unimaginable torment (see *plate 25*). That, though, is only half the surprise. As our eyes wander across this landscape of Medieval eschatology, they stop at last in the relative obscurity of the bottom left quadrant of the mural. There, to our further astonishment, a devil stirs a boiling cauldron full of people and glares straight at us as he does so. And there the joke is complete. We, too, are and always were part of this mural, bonded to it by the eyes of a devil, the same eyes that watched us walk up the aisle, admire the altar and font, and bask in the antique light.

The Chaldon mural, for all its superficial humor, is one of the more spectacular examples of the *memento mori* tradition. Its purpose was

similar to that of the plethora of death's head and *danse macabre* art
spawned in early modern times. The observer had to be reminded of his
spiritual imperatives, and encouraged to change his ways accordingly.
The intention was not simply to inform but to *re*form; to urge the pilgrim
to a better life and, thence, to a better afterlife. "This could be you in the
pot!" the demon seems to be saying as he stares at us. To a world that
believed implicitly in the boiling pots of hell, it was no frivolous warning.

Shakespeare's England also believed in the boiling pots of hell but
instead of spurring its inhabitants to greater piety that thought seems
almost to have had the effect of encouraging them to a greater celebration
of earthly existence. Typically, this did not represent itself in the
extravagant festivity of life, with a commensurate repudiation of the
afterlife, proposed by D'Amville in *The Atheist's Tragedy*:

> Then, if Death casts up
> Our total sum of joy and happiness,
> Let me have all my senses feasted in
> The abundant fulness of delight at once,
> And, with a sweet insensible increase
> Of pleasing surfeit, melt into my dust.
>   (I.i.17-22)[1]

More usually, it took the form of a poignant and moving nostalgia for
life on earth, often expressed within the religious context of memorial
plaques and tombs. Consider, for example, the alabaster detail of a
young man picking fruit on a marble column in the 1532 de la Warr
funereal chantry at Boxgrove Priory. The youth clambers up a tree,
young and alive, and casts down apples to a maiden on the ground who
gathers them up in her apron (see *plate 26*). Who were these young
people? No precise answer is intended: you, me, any person who was or
is in the full flush of life. In the simple details of ordinary mortality, in
the joys of youth and the redolent memories of old age, we perceive the
reason for existence, the value of "being."

In the first chapter of this book I suggested that Shakespeare's theatre
asked a question of seminal importance. If earthly life is worthless, and
the only truly valuable existence is the spiritual incarnation after death,
then what is the point of earthly life? Shakespeare experimented with
this tension in various ways. Secularizing familiar life-in-death images,
in the manner of his English contemporaries and literary antecedents,

Shakespeare set out in the Histories to construct a wondrous English myth, based on a combination of civil peace and foreign military greatness, and renewing itself from generation to generation. Yet, his theatre, even while espousing the model of an English paradise, is never entirely comfortable with the life-in-death paradigm. The initial problem was the English propensity for civil war, recounted assiduously in the chronicle sources of Shakespeare's earliest historical works. And luckily, or perhaps unluckily, the recurrent blight of civil war in the English historical landscape fell rather neatly into the life-in-death mold. Throughout the history plays, and even in *Henry V*, glorious revivification is disturbingly undermined by the insidious revivification of civil ailments. It is not this discordant mirroring, though, that finally obstructs Shakespeare's experiment with the life-in-death motif as a remedy for the transience of mortal life. Rather, it is the nature of "glorious foreign conquest" itself that destroys the hope that death can be defeated by the idea of one chivalric generation physically procreating the next.

At the same time as Shakespeare was experimenting with the life-in-death theme he began to explore, as well, the potential of *memento mori* motifs as theatrical emblems. Images of skulls, representations of decaying cadavers and the *danse macabre* were recognizable and "ready-made" icons in church and funerary art. They offered skeins of meaning that had been exploited in dramatic contexts since the fourteenth century, and Shakespeare probed their possibilities in various ways throughout his career. Some of his usage may be deemed normative in the sense that he takes a familiar device and transposes it, meaning and all, into a theatrical context. The idea of antic Death as a leveler; the notion of the grave as a release from the mortal coil; the antithesis between dead bone and living flesh — all of these appear fairly routinely throughout the canon. His more interesting developments include, for example, the fusion of mortality and the dance of death in a character like Coriolanus whose superlative warriorship bestows upon him, at least for a time, the mantle of the Death soldier. Similarly, it is apparent in the dance of death animation of Richard II's murder which succeeds in forcing us, as the audience, to refocus our impression of the king and his stature.

The History plays largely construe death as a physical moment in time, a catastrophic watershed between mortal life and something else. The "trumping" of death through heroic physical renewal (progeny) and memory (recollection of past greatness) is deemed a process of utmost urgency. In the patriarchal world of *Romeo and Juliet*, love and death have been drawn into a scheme of sin and punishment, their traditional cosmic jurisdiction apparently subjected to the mortal control of the play's authority figures.   Such subjugation is illusory and its hollowness is reiterated by the untimely death of youth, culminating in the fall of Romeo and Juliet.   Linked to the *de morte et amore* iconic *topos*, the play's manipulation of images of youth and age perhaps informs the outcome of the drama, suggesting that such tragedies are at once incomprehensible and inevitable.   But it is one thing to acknowledge that which is inescapable, quite another to cope with the idea of one's own personal death.   *Hamlet* begins and ends with death central to its visual vigor but, unlike *Romeo and Juliet*, the inquiry looks more to the individual than to his social milieu, its purposes more personally reflective than socially restorative. Hamlet, the man, must come to terms with his own mortality and the death's head, specifically Yorick's skull, is instrumental to this end. The rituals of deathly contemplation, funereal loitering, *memento mori*, even the mimicking of the *danse macabre,* seem somehow to enlighten and sustain him as he stares finally into the face of extinction.

Note

1. Cyril Tourneur, *The Atheist's Tragedy* in *John Webster and Cyril Tourneur: Four Plays*, ed. John Addington Symonds (New York: Hill and Wang, 1966).

Plates

ॐ

Plate 1: The back panel of an early sixteenth century arm chair in the private collection of the Red Lion Hotel (named the White Bear Inn in Medieval times), Salisbury, Wiltshire. Note that Adam and Eve hold hands (or are they, in fact, mischievously sharing a forbidden fruit?) — an interesting celebration of human love in the face of the greatest crime ever committed on earth.

Plate 2: A winged child reclines upon a skull in the memorial to Anne Markham (died 1601) in the Parish Church of St. Mary Magdalene at Newark-on-Trent in Nottinghamshire. Such motifs were common on gravestones and other funereal monuments, reminding all and sundry that even the most youthful and beautiful would physically wither and perish.

Plate 3: "The Bride," in Hans Holbein's *Imagines Mortis* (Lyon, 1545), sig. C4r. In later editions, it is specifically the bride who is being drummed to the grave by Death. The marriage to Death was a familiar and ancient theme by the time it reached Shakespeare's age. It is reiterated in the *danse macabre* representation in the de la Warr Chantry (see *plate 20*) and even perhaps in the panel at the Parish Church of St. Mary Magdalene at Newark-on-Trent (see *plate 17*) as Death offers a carnation to her (?) intended paramour. Reproduced by courtesy of Glasgow University Library, Special Collections Department (SM 202.1).

Plates

Plate 4: A death's head clock, carved by Spanish prisoners after the débâcle of the Spanish Armada in 1588, and still housed in The White Bear Inn (now called the Red Lion Hotel), a Medieval inn house in Salisbury, Wiltshire. The original mechanisms of the clock have been long lost. The clock face and movement were made in Plymouth in the early years of the nineteenth century and the organ is thought to be German, from around about the same time. When the organ is set in motion, the skeletons ring the bells above them. Many of the carved figures on the case reflect Iberian fashions of the time but the death's head warning at the top of the clock was a symbol every sixteenth century European would have understood.

Plate 5: Aeneas saving his father, Anchises, from the burning ruins of Troy. The episode was held as a consummate illustration of filial loyalty and also played on the idea of one generation inheriting its strengths and values from the preceding generation. From Geffrey Whitney's *A Choice of Emblemes* (Leyden, 1586), p. 163, the most popular English emblem book of the sixteenth century. The print derived originally from the work of Alciati. Reproduced by courtesy of Glasgow University Library, Special Collections Department (SM 1667).

Plate 6: Adam and Eve, after their expulsion from paradise. A skeletal death assists Adam to lever a root, a sign of the mortality and hard labor of the fallen world. In the background, smiling Eve nurses her first born. From Holbein's *Icones Historiarvm Veteris Testamenti* (Lyon, 1547), sig. B1v. By permission of the British Library (3128 c 29).

Spes altera vitæ.
Hope of another life.

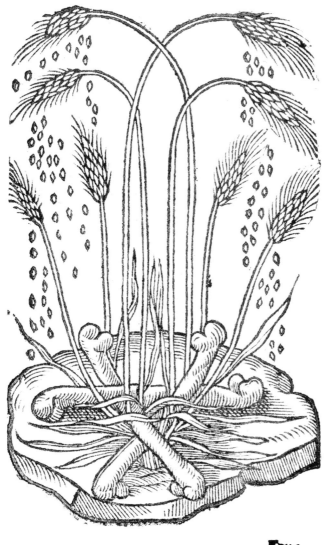

Fru

Plate 7: "Hope of another life" from the English version of Claude Paradin's *Heroicall Devises* (London, 1591), p. 320. Seeds fall from what appear to be wheat plants, landing amongst bones, offering the prospect of life generating from the "fertility" of death. The meaning was preeminently religious but expressed in tangibly physical terms. By permission of the British Library (264 a 24).

*Death is no Loſſe, but rather, Gaine ;
For wee by Dying, Life attaine.*

ILLVSTR. XXI.   Book. I.

Plate 8: George Wither's print of life in death reveals sprigs of wheat growing out of the eye sockets of a death's head. From *A Collection of Emblemes* (London, 1635), p. 21. Again, the print signifies the idea of spiritual life superseding physical death — a religious significance iterated through physical imagery. Reproduced by courtesy of Glasgow University Library, Special Collections Department (SM 1903).

Plate 9: Detail from a seventeenth century wall tapestry in the Royal Chambers at Hampton Court Palace, London. The Hydra, by every account a monstrous beast, is dwarfed by Hercules in the central panel of the tapestry (on the right of the picture), indicating the hero's moral superiority over the forces of evil.

Plate 10: The so-called Wakeman Cenotaph at Tewkesbury Abbey, Gloucestershire — though many believe that Abbot Wakeman's body does not, in fact, reside here. The fifteenth century alabaster cadaver has several sculpted worms crawling on or beside it, as well as vermin burrowing into the chest cavity and elsewhere. A worm is visible on the left knee; and you may just be able to see a marble rodent gnawing at the left arm.

Plate 11: In this sixteenth century *memento mori* brass plaque on the floor of St. Andrew's Church, Oddington, Oxfordshire, worms crawl through the cavities of a shrouded skeleton. The piece commemorates one Ralph Hamsterley but the fact that the date of his death is not included on the inscription suggests that it was made at Hamsterley's behest while he was still alive. Three other copies of the plaque are known to have existed, one of which resided at Merton College, Oxford, but only that in St. Andrew's Church has survived.

Plate 12:   Geffrey Whitney's print of Cupid and Death in *A Choice of Emblemes* (Leyden, 1586), p. 132, was merely a slight variation on a familiar emblem book theme. Interestingly, though, the title of Whitney's print, "De morte, et amore: Iocosum" (Of death and love: a humorous tale), suggests that he saw the episode in a rather more jocular fashion than other emblematists. Reproduced by courtesy of Glasgow University Library, Special Collections Department (SM 1667).

Plate 13: "De Morte, et Cupidne," from Henry Peacham's *Minerva Britanna* (London, 1612), p. 172. Peacham's was the first emblem book by an Englishman to have its first edition published in England. The artistic skills of English woodcutters lagged behind their continental counterparts, as suggested by the clear but rather unsophisticated lines of the print above. Reproduced by courtesy of Glasgow University Library, Special Collections Department (SM 829).

Plate 14: In these carvings on marble columns in the de la Warr Chapel Chantry at Boxgrove Priory, West Sussex, Cupid is presented in varying guises. In the first, he holds a flower in his right hand and a fish in his left — signifying, as in Andrea Alciati's print "Vis Amoris," from *Emblematvm Libellvs* (Paris, 1534), his power over all living things, be they on land or sea. In the second, he strums a lute — a symbol of harmony and lovers' songs. The Chantry was constructed in 1532.

Plate 15: At St. Mary's Church at Patrixbourne, Kent, a late sixteenth century stained glass window recounts the tragic story of Pyramus and Thisbe. Thisbe cries out with grief at the sight of her lover, impaled on a sword. Below, Cupidesque figures play with hoops, oblivious of the condition to which love has brought the unfortunate couple.

Plate 16: "Vis Amoris," from Andrea Alciati's *Emblemi di Andrea Alciato* (Padua, 1626), p. 155. The emblem illustrates the proverbial power of love, depicting the child-like Cupid breaking a thunderbolt in two. Reproduced by courtesy of Glasgow University Library, Special Collections Department (SM 71).

Plate 17: This early-Renaissance (c. 1520) dance of death painting in the Markham Chantry at the Parish Church of St. Mary Magdalene, Newark-on-Trent, Nottinghamshire, is the only surviving panel of a series that once circuited the chantry. The detail shows a grinning *danse macabre* figure offering a red carnation to a fashionably dressed young man (out of picture). One hand holds the flower, the other gestures pointedly to the grave. The young man clasps his purse, a sign of his obsession with earthly things. The lesson is simple: all that lives must die and the treasures of the world will be of no use in the grave.

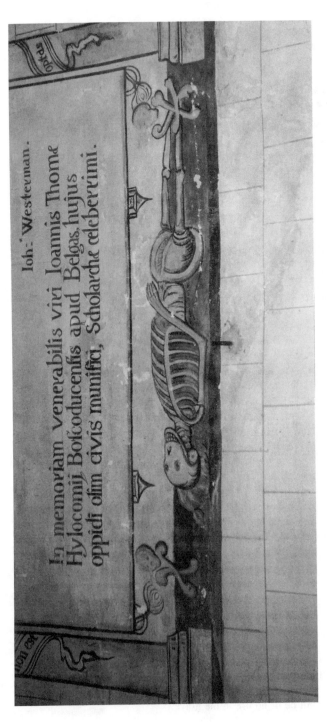

Plate 18: The "skeleton" of John Thomas Hylocomius (who died in January 1595), with verse accompaniment, at St. Alban's Cathedral, Hertfordshire. A continental visitor who stayed longer than he expected, Hylocomius was so revered by his students that they united to provide a memorial for him in the cathedral. And so, the epitaph advises, although the great master is now no more than a "mere shade" the memory of his scholarship and learning will endure. On the outskirts of London, and situated in a popular hostelry town on the route to Stratford-on-Avon and the west of England, St. Alban's would probably have been well-known to Shakespeare.

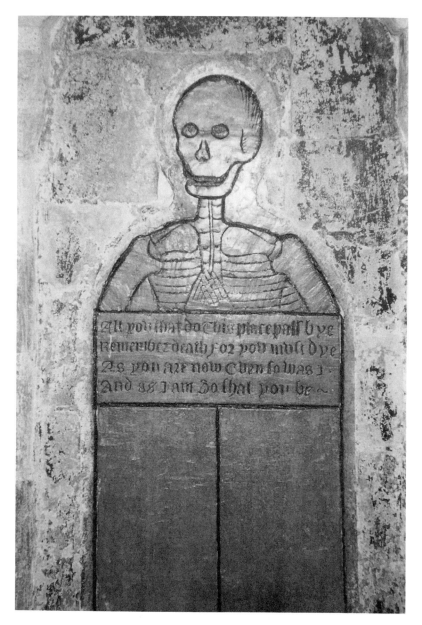

Plate 19: The late sixteenth century funeral memorial to John Gooding in Norwich Cathedral, portraying a grinning skeleton, his hands clasped mockingly in prayer. He looks directly at us, the viewers, taunting the transience of our mortality and mimicking the sometimes shallow spirituality of the world through his own caricature of piety.

174 *Plates*

Plate 20: A dance of death figure reaches for the hand of a reticent young maiden on an exterior column of the early sixteenth century de la Warr Chantry at Boxgrove Priory, West Sussex. Death ominously holds a spade in his right hand, a familiar agrarian emblem of mortality. At the Dissolution, Henry VIII proposed to destroy the Priory but local people were able to raise enough money to buy him off. However, the de la Warr family, who had built the chantry for their own entombment, were ultimately denied that right.

Plate 21: "Mors sceptra ligonibus aequans," from Simeoni's *Pvrtratvres Or Emblemes of Gabriel Simeon, a Florentine* (London, 1591), p. 373 — wrongly numbered as p. 273 in the 1591 edition. The death's head reminds the observer that the royal scepter and the poor man's mattock are equal in the eyes of death, and the prose accompaniment affirms the function of death as a universal leveler. By permission of the British Library (264 a 24).

," in Hans Holbein's *Imagines Mortis* (Lyon, 1545), sig.
ises his absolute power over abject subjects but Death, the
wings ready to reduce royalty to the same state as a
ly seems to be delving into the Emperor's head —
nenting his mind before snatching his physical life too (a
in the allusions to Death at the end of *King John*).
Glasgow University Library, Special Collections

Plate 21: "Mors sceptra ligonibus aequans," from Simeoni's *Pvrtratvres Or Emblemes of Gabriel Simeon, a Florentine* (London, 1591), p. 373 — wrongly numbered as p. 273 in the 1591 edition. The death's head reminds the observer that the royal scepter and the poor man's mattock are equal in the eyes of death, and the prose accompaniment affirms the function of death as a universal leveler. By permission of the British Library (264 a 24).

Plate 22: "The Emperor," in Hans Holbein's *Imagines Mortis* (Lyon, 1545), sig. A6r. The emperor exercises his absolute power over abject subjects but Death, the great leveler, waits in the wings ready to reduce royalty to the same state as a pauper. Death here actually seems to be delving into the Emperor's head — perhaps in the hope of tormenting his mind before snatching his physical life too (a process that seems evident in the allusions to Death at the end of *King John*). Reproduced by courtesy of Glasgow University Library, Special Collections Department (SM 202.1).

Plate 23: An old man steps out of an orb, aided by a sympathetic Death figure, in Georgette de Montenay's *Emblematvm Christianorvm Centvria* (Zurich, 1584), p. 89r. The orb represents the world, which is suitably hollow to represent the insubstantiality of earthly things. A Latin motto suggests that Death is here a welcome visitor to an old man who desires death as an end to mortal suffering. Reproduced by courtesy of Glasgow University Library, Special Collections Department (SM 772).

Plate 24: Gabriel Simeoni's figure of merciless wickedness in *Pvrtratvres Or Emblemes of Gabriel Simeon, a Florentine* (London: William Kearney, 1591), p. 364. The sense of "lesson" implicit in the emblem books is here illustrated by the fact that the Death figure looks not at his victim but at us. By permission of the British Library (264 a 24).

Plate 25: "The Road to Heaven," a Medieval mural in the Church of St. Peter and St. Paul, Chaldon, on the so-called "Pilgrim's Way" from London to Canterbury, and just a few miles south from where the Globe Theatre stood. The demon who gazes out at us in the bottom left quadrant is busy stirring the "The Murderer's Pot," a term used frequently in the sixteenth and earlier centuries to designate one of hell's most excruciating torments.

Plate 26: A detail from the 1532 de la Warr Chapel Chantry in Boxgrove Priory, West Sussex. A young man climbs a tree to collect fruits while a maiden gathers them up in her apron on the ground below. The image serves to celebrate the simple joys and pleasures of human life.

List of References

Alciati, Andrea. *Andreas Alciatus. 1: The Latin Emblems, Indexes and Lists.* Ed. Peter M. Daly, with Virginia W. Callahan and assisted by Simon Cuttler. Toronto: U of Toronto P, 1985.

———. *Andreas Alciatus. 2: Emblems in Translation: Index Emblematicus.* Ed. Peter M. Daly, assisted by Simon Cuttler. Toronto: U of Toronto P, 1985.

———. *Emblemata.* Padua: Tozzi, 1621.

———. *Emblematvm Libellvs.* Paris: Christian Wechel, 1534.

———. *Emblemi di Andrea Alciato.* Padua: Tozzi, 1626.

Anderson, M.D. *History and Imagery in British Churches.* London: John Murray, 1995.

Ariès, Philippe. *Western Attitudes toward Death: From the Middle Ages to the Present.* Trans. Patricia M. Ranum. Baltimore: The Johns Hopkins UP, 1974.

Bache, William B. and Vernon P. Loggins. *Shakespeare's Deliberate Art.* Lanham: The UP of America, 1996.

Bache, William B. *Design and Closure in Shakespeare's Major Plays: The Nature of Recapitulation.* New York: Peter Lang, 1991.

Banister, John. *Historie of Man, sucked from the sappe of the most approued Anathomistes.* London: 1578.

Bartsch, Adam. *Le Peintre Graveur.* Leipzig: J.A. Barth, 1866.

Batman, Stephen. *The Golden Booke of the Leaden Goddes.* 1577. New York: Garland, 1976.

Beaumont, Francis. *The Knight of the Burning Pestle.* Ed. Andrew Gurr. Berkeley: The U of California P, 1966.

Bennett, Josephine Waters. "Britain Among The Fortunate Isles." *Studies in Philology* 53 (1956): 114-40.

Black, Matthew W., ed. *A New Variorum Edition of Shakespeare: The Life and Death of King Richard the Second.* Philadelphia: Lippincott, 1955.

Bliss, Lee. "The Wheel of Fortune and the Maiden Phoenix of Shakespeare's King Henry the Eighth." *ELH* 42 (1975): 1-25.

Bocchi, Achille. *Symbolicarum Quaestionum, De vniuerso genere, quas serio ludebat, Libri Qvinqve.* 1555. Bononiae: apud Societatem Typographiae Bononiensis, 1574.

Bry, Theodore de. *Emblemata.* Frankfurt am Main: 1593.

Bullough, Geoffrey, ed. *Narrative and Dramatic Sources of Shakespeare*, Vol. 3. London: Routledge & Kegan Paul, 1960.

Calderwood, James L. *Shakespeare and the Denial of Death.* Amherst: U of Massachusetts P, 1987.

Carlin, Patricia L. *Shakespeare's Mortal Men: Overcoming Death in History, Comedy and Tragedy.* New York: Peter Lang, 1993.

Cartari, Vincenzo. *Le Imagini de i Dei de gli Antichi.* Venice: 1571.

Caxton, William. *Chronycles of Englande*. St. Albans: 1483.

Chamberlain, Arthur B. *Hans Holbein The Younger*. 2 vols. London: George Allen, 1913.

Chew, Samuel C. *The Pilgrimage of Life*. 1962. Port Washington: Kennikat, 1973.

Cho, Kwang Soon. *Emblems in Shakespeare's Last Plays*. Lanham: UP of America, 1998.

Cooper, Geoffrey and Christopher Wortham, eds. *Everyman*. Nedlands: U of Western Australia P, 1980.

Cooper, Thomas. *Thesavrvs Lingvae Romanae & Britannicae tam accurate congestus, vt nihil pene in eo desyderari possit, quod vel Latine complectatur amplissimus Stephani Thesaurus, vel Anglice, toties aucta Eliotae Bibliotheca*. London: 1565.

Daly, Peter, with Leslie T. Duer and Anthony Raspa, eds. *The English Emblem Tradition*. Vol. 1. Toronto: U of Toronto P, 1988.

Daly, Peter. Introduction. In *The English Emblem Tradition*. Vol. 2. Ed. Peter M. Daly, with Leslie T. Duer and Mary V. Silcox. Toronto: U of Toronto P, 1993. xi-xvii.

Daniel, Samuel. *Delia. Contayning certayne sonnets: with the complaint of Rosamond*. London: J. Charlwood for Simon Waterson, 1592.

———. *The Civile Wares betweene the Howses of Lancaster and Yorke*. 1595. London: Simon Waterson, 1609

Danse Macabre. Troyes: after 1500.

Davis, Philip. *Sudden Shakespeare: The Shaping of Shakespeare's Creative Thought*. London: Athlone, 1996.

Daza, Bernardino. *Emblemas*. Lyon: Bonhomme, 1549.

Dekker, Thomas. *The Shoemakers' Holiday*. In *Elizabethan and Jacobean Comedies: A New Mermaid Anthology*. Ed. D. J. Palmer. Tonbridge, Kent: Ernest Benn, 1984.

Diehl, Huston, ed. *English Emblem Books, 1500-1700*. Norman: U of Oklahoma P, 1986.

Doebler, John. *Shakespeare's Speaking Pictures: Studies in Iconic Imagery*. Albuquerque: U of New Mexico P, 1974.

Donne, John. "Death's Duell, or, A Consolation to the Soule against the dying Life and living Death of the Body." *Selections from Divine Poems, Sermons, Devotions, and Prayers*. Ed. John Booty. New York: Paulist, 1990. 233-50.

Du Bartas, Guillaume de Salluste. *Du Bartas. His Diuine Weekes and Workes with A Compleate Collectiō of all the other most delight-full Workes*. Trans. Joshua Sylvester. London: 1605.

Dundas, Judith. "The Masks of Cupid and Death." *Comparative Drama* 29 (1995): 38-60.

Engel, William E. *Mapping Mortality: The Persistence of Memory and Melancholy in Early Modern England*. Amherst: U of Massachusetts P, 1995.

Eruditorium penitentiale. Paris: Antoine Caillaut, 1480.

Farrell, Kirby. *Play, Death, and Heroism in Shakespeare*. Chapel Hill: The U of North Carolina P, 1989.

Foakes, R. A. *Hamlet Versus Lear: Cultural Politics and Shakespeare's Art*. Cambridge: Cambridge UP, 1993.

Folland, Harold F. "King Richard's Pallid Victory." *Shakespeare Quarterly* 24 (1973): 390-9.

Fowler, Alastair. *Time's Purpled Masquers: Stars and the Afterlife in Renaissance English Literature*. Oxford: Clarendon, 1996.

Freeman, Rosemary. *English Emblem Books*. 1948. London: Chatto & Windus, 1967.

Frye, Roland Mushat. *The Renaissance Hamlet: Issues and Responses in 1600*. Princeton: Princeton UP, 1984.

Geoffrey of Monmouth, *Historia Britonum*. 1136-8 (?). Ed. J. A. Giles. London: D. Nutt, 1844.

Gerould, G. H. "King Arthur and Politics." *Speculum* 2 (1927): 33-51.

Gough, Lionel. *A Short Guide to the Abbey Church of St. Mary the Virgin at Tewkesbury*. 5th ed. Tewkesbury: Friends of Tewkesbury Abbey, 1991.

Green, Henry. *Shakespeare and the Emblem Writers*. London: Trubner, 1870.

Hall, Edward. *The Vnion of the two noble and illustre famelies of Lancastre & Yorke*. 1548. London: Richard Grafton, 1584.

Hallett, Charles A. and Elaine S. Hallett. *Analyzing Shakespeare's Action: Scene versus Sequence*. Cambridge: Cambridge UP, 1991.

Hawley, William M. *Critical Hermeneutics and Shakespeare's History Plays*. New York: Peter Lang, 1992.

Holbein, Hans. *The Dance of Death*. Ed. James M. Clark. London: Phaidon, 1947.

———. *Icones Historiarvm Veteris Testamenti*. Lvgdvni: apud Ioannem Frellonium, 1547.

———. *The Images of the Old Testament*. Lyon: Johan Frellon, 1549.

———. *Imagines Mortis*. 1538 (as *Les Simulachres & Historiees faces de la Mort, avtant elegammet pourtraictes, que artificiellement imaginées*). Lyon: Trechsel, 1545.

Holinshed, Raphael. *Holinshed's Chronicle*. 1577. Ed. Allardyce & Josephine Nicoll. London: Dent, 1965.

Hunger, Wolfgang. *Emblemata*. Paris: Christian Wechel, 1542.

Hyland, Peter. *An Introduction to Shakespeare*. New York: St. Martin's, 1996.

Ijsewijn, Jozef. "A Latin Death-dance play of 1532." *Humanistica Lovaniensia: Journal of Neo-Latin Studies* 18 (1969): 77-94.

Janson, Horst W. "A 'Memento Mori' among early Italian Prints." *Journal of the Warburg and Cortauld Institutes* 3 (1939-40): 243-8.

Jones, John. *Shakespeare at Work*. Oxford: Clarendon, 1995.

Jourdan, Silvester. *A Plaine Description of the Barmvdas, now called Sommer Ilands*. London: W. Stansby for W. Welby, 1613.

Kiernan, Pauline. *Shakespeare's Theory of Drama*. Cambridge: Cambridge UP, 1996.

A Knack to Know a Knave. 1594. Oxford: The Malone Society Reprints, 1963.

Kyd, Thomas. *The Spanish Tragedy*. Ed. J. R. Mulryne. *Elizabethan and Jacobean Tragedies: A New Mermaid Anthology*. Introduced by Brian Gibbons. Tonbridge: Ernest Benn, 1984.

Latimer, Hugh. *Seven Sermons made vpon the Lordes Prayer*. London: John Day, 1571.

Lefèvre, Jehan. *Emblèmes*. Paris: Christian Wechel, 1536.

Leigh, Gerard. *The Accedence of Armorie*. 1562. London: R. Tottel, 1591.

Lemprière's Classical Dictionary of Proper Names mentioned in Ancient Authors. Ed. F. A. Wright. London: Routledge & Kegan Paul, 1978.

Lerner, Robert E., Standish Meacham, and Edward McNall Burns, *Western Civilizations: Their History and Their Culture*. 12th ed. New York: W. W. Norton, 1993.

Levith, Murray J. *Shakespeare's Italian Settings and Plays*. New York: St. Martin's, 1989.

Linche, Richard. *The Fovntaine of Ancient Fiction*. 1599. New York: Garland, 1976.

Llewellyn, Nigel. *The Art of Death: Visual Culture in the English Death Ritual c. 1500 - c. 1800*. London: Reaktion Books, in association with the Victoria and Albert Museum, 1991.

Lodge, Thomas. *The Wounds of Civil War*. 1594. Ed. Joseph W. Houppert. London: Edward Arnold, 1969.

MacKenzie, Clayton G. "Falstaff's Monster." *AUMLA: Journal of the Australasian Universities Modern Languages Association* 83 (1995): 83-6.

———. "Paradise and Paradise Lost in *Richard II*." *Shakespeare Quarterly* 37 (1986): 318-39.

Mâle, Emile. *L'Art Religieux de la fin du Moyen Âge en France*. Paris: Librairie Armand Colin, 1908.

Maley, Willy. "'This sceptred isle': Shakespeare and the British problem." *Shakespeare and National Culture*. Ed. John J. Joughin. Manchester: Manchester UP, 1997. 83-108.

Marchant, Guyot. *Danse macabre*. Paris: 1485.

Marlowe, Christopher. *The Complete Plays*. Ed. J. B. Steane. Harmondsworth: Penguin, 1973.

Marnix van Sant Aldegonde, Philips van. *A Tragicall Historie of the troubles and Ciuile Warres of the lowe Countries, otherwise called Flanders*. Trans. Thomas Stocker. London: J. Kyngston for T. Smith, 1583.

Marquale, Giovanni. *Imprese*. Lyon: Bonhomme, 1551.

Marston, John. *The Malcontent and Other Plays*. Ed. Keith Sturgess. Oxford: Oxford UP, 1997.

Mason, H. A. *Shakespeare's Tragedies of Love*. New York: Barnes & Noble, 1970.

Massinger, Philip. *A New Way To Pay Old Debts*. *Four Jacobean City Comedies*. Ed. Gamini Salgado. Harmondsworth: Penguin, 1985.

McNatt, Glenn. "Cambodians stare at us, and ask why they must die." *The Baltimore Sun*. Internet edition. Online. 27 July 1997.

Middleton, Thomas and William Rowley. *The Changeling*. Ed. N. W. Bawcutt. Manchester: Manchester UP, 1994.

Middleton, Thomas. *A Chaste Maid in Cheapside*. Ed. Alan Brissenden. London: Ernest Benn, 1974.

The Mirror for Magistrates. 1555. Ed. Lily B. Campbell. New York: Barnes & Noble, 1960.

Montenay, Georgette de. *Emblematvm Christianorvm Centvria*. 1571. Zurich, 1584.

More, Thomas. *Utopia*. 1516, Latin version; 1547, English version. Ed. Edward Surtz. New Haven: Yale UP, 1964.

Morris, Harry. "The Dance of Death Motif in Shakespeare." *Papers on Language and Literature: A Journal for Scholars and Critics of Language and Literature* 20 (1984): 15-28.

———. *Last Things in Shakespeare*. Tallahassee: Florida State UP, 1985.

Moseley, Charles. *A Century of Emblems: An Introductory Anthology*. Aldershot: Scolar, 1989.

Neill, Michael. "'Exeunt with a Dead March': Funeral Pageantry on the Shakespearean Stage." *Pageantry in the Shakespearean Theater*. Ed. David M. Bergeron. Athens: U of Georgia P, 1985. 153-93.

———. *Issues of Death: Mortality and Identity in English Renaissance Tragedy*. Oxford: Clarendon, 1997.

Newton, Eric. *Tintoretto*. London: Longmans, Green, 1952.

Oman, C. W. C. *The Art of War in the Middle Ages*. 1885. Ithaca: Cornell UP, 1993.

Paradin, Claude. *Les Devises Heroiques*. 1551. Anvers: 1561.

———. *The Heroicall Devises of M. Clavdivs Paradin Canon of Beauieu, whereunto are added the Lord Gabriel Symeons and others*. Trans. P.S. London: William Kearney, 1591.

Peacham, Henry. *Minerva Britanna: Or A Garden of Heroycal Devices*. London: Wa. Dight, 1612.

Peckham, G. *A Trve Report, Of the late discoueries, and possession, taken in the right of the Crowne of Englande, of the New-found Landes*. London: 1583.

Perrière, Guillaume de la. *La Morosophie de Guillaume de la Perriere Tolosain, Contenant Cent Emblemes moraux.* Lyon: Bonhomme, 1553.

———. *Le Theatre des bons engins auquel sont contenuz cent Emblemes moraulx.* Paris, 1539.

———. *The Theater of fine devices, containing an hundred morall emblemes.* Trans. Thomas Combe. 1593. London: R. Field, 1614.

Phillipps, Evelyn March. *Tintoretto.* London: Methuen, 1911.

Pliny (Plinius Secundus). *The Secrets and wonders of the worlde. A booke ryght rare and straunge, contayning many excellent properties, giuen to Man, Beastes, Foules, fishes, and Serpents, Trees and Plants.* London: T. Hacket, 1587.

Potter, Lois. "The Antic Disposition of Richard II." *Shakespeare Survey* 27 (1974): 33-41.

Price, Daniel. *Lamentations for the death of the late Illustrious Prince Henry: and the dissolution of his religious Familie.* London: Tho. Snodham for R. Jackson, 1613.

Pugliatti, Paola. *Shakespeare the Historian.* New York: St. Martin's, 1996.

Quarles, Francis. *Emblemes.* London: J. Williams, 1634.

Rabkin, Norman. *Shakespeare and the Common Understanding.* New York: Free Press, 1967.

Raleigh, Walter. *Selections from his Writings.* Ed. G. E. Hadow. Oxford: Clarendon, 1917.

Rastell, John. *The Pastyme of the People The Chronycles of dyuers realmys and most specyally of the realme of England.* London: 1529.

Reusner, Nicholas. *Emblemata Nicolai Revsneri.* Frankfurt: 1581.

Rougemont, Denis de. *Love in the Western World.* Trans. Montgomery Belgion. New York: Pantheon, 1956.

Sambucus, Joannes. *Emblemata, cum aliquot nummis antiqui operis, Ioannis Sambuci Tirnaviensis Pannonii.* Antwerp: Christopher Plantin, 1564.

Saviolo, Vincentio. *His Practise. In two Bookes. The first intreating of the vse of the Rapier and Dagger. The second, of Honour and Honourable Quarrels.* London: T. Scarlet for J. Wolfe, 1595.

Schedel, Hartman. *Liber Chronicum.* ("The Chronicle of Nuremberg"). Nuremberg: 1493.

Shakespeare, William. *King Henry V.* Ed. John H. Walter. London: Methuen, 1970.

———. *The Riverside Shakespeare,* 2nd ed. Eds. G. Blakemore Evans et al. Boston: Houghton Mifflin, 1997.

Simeoni, Gabriel. *Pvrtratvres Or Emblemes of Gabriel Simeon, a Florentine.* In *The Heroicall Devises of M. Clavdivs Paradin Canon of Beauieu, whereunto are added the Lord Gabriel Symeons and others.* Trans. P.S. London: William Kearney, 1591.

Simonds, Peggy Muñoz. *Myth, Emblem, and Music in Shakespeare's Cymbeline: An Iconographic Reconstruction.* Newark: U of Delaware P, 1992.

Spencer, Theodore. *Death in Elizabethan Tragedy: A Study of Convention and Opinion in the Elizabethan Drama.* 1936. New York: Pageant Books, 1960

Spenser, Edmund. *The Faerie Queene.* 1590. Ed. Thomas P. Roche. Harmondsworth: Penguin, 1978.

Stilling, Roger. *Love and Death in Renaissance Tragedy.* Baton Rouge: Louisiana State UP, 1976.

Sutcliffe, Matthew. *The Practice, Proceedings, And Lawes of armes, described out of the doings of most valiant and expert Captaines, and confirmed both by ancient, and moderne examples, and praecedents.* London: Christopher Barker, 1593.

Taylor, Jane H. M. "The Dialogues of the Dance of Death and the Limits of Late-Medieval Theatre." *Fifteenth Century Studies* 16 (1990): 215-32.

Tertio, Francesco. *Austriacae Gentis Imagines.* 1558. Venetiis et Oeniponti: Formis Gaspari ab Avibus, 1573.

Tourneur, Cyril. *The Atheist's Tragedy.* In *John Webster and Cyril Tourneur: Four Plays.* Ed. John Addington Symonds. New York: Hill & Wang, 1966.

Walsh, Martin W. "'This same skull, Sir . . .': Layers of Meaning and Tradition in Shakespeare's most famous Prop." *Hamlet Studies: An International Journal of Research on the Tragedie of Hamlet, Prince of Denmarke* (New Delhi, India) 9 (1987): 65-77.

Watson, Elizabeth See. *Achille Bocchi and the Emblem Book as Symbolic Form.* Cambridge: Cambridge UP, 1993.

Watson, Robert. *The Rest Is Silence: Death as Annihilation in the English Renaissance.* Berkeley: U of California P, 1994.

Webster, John. *The White Devil.* Ed. John Russell Brown. Manchester: Manchester UP, 1992).

Whitney, Geffrey. *A Choice of Emblemes.* Leyden: Christopher Plantin, 1586.

Willet, Andrew. *Sacrorum Emblematum Centuria Una.* London: 1592.

Wimpheling, Jacob. *Adolescentia.* Strasbourg: Martin Flach, 1500.

Wind, Edgar. *Pagan Mysteries in the Renaissance.* Rev. ed. Oxford: Oxford UP, 1980.

Wither, George. *A Collection of Emblemes, Ancient and Moderne.* 1635. Ed. Rosemary Freeman. Columbia: U of South Carolina P, 1975.

Wymer, Rowland. *Suicide and Despair in the Jacobean Drama.* Brighton: Harvester, 1986.

Wyrley, William. *The Trve Vse of Armorie, Shewed by Historie, and plainly proued by example.* London: J. Jackson for Gabriell Cawood, 1592.

Index

Page references in *italics* indicate plates. References followed by 'n' indicate endnotes.

Wimpheling, Jacob, 146n50, 187; *Adolescentia,* 137
Wind, Edgar, 89n1, 187
Wither, George, 29, 187; *A Collection of Emblemes, Ancient and Moderne,* 38n38, 122, 145n27; "Death is no Losse, but rather, Gaine," *162*
Wolgemut, Michael, 117, 130
worms, 49

Wortham, Christopher, 143n7, 182
Wright, F. A., 146n47, 184
Wymer, Roland, 84, 92n36, 187
Wyrley, William, 18, 36n11, 51, 63n28, 187

Yorick's skull, 100; Hamlet's contemplation of, 6, 95, 104-9, 114n31, 150
A Young Man with a Skull (Hals), 95